LIVING THE BEATITUDES

FAST LANE BIBLE STUDIES

by Abe Bergen

Faith & Life Press, Newton, Kansas

ACKNOWLEDGEMENTS

As part of a Grade 9 religion project at Westgate Mennonite Collegiate in Winnipeg, Manitoba, Jeremy Bergen (in 1990) and Rachel Bergen (in 1993) wrote the stories in the "Apply" movements. Their instructor was Werner Wiens.

Norma Peters Duerksen, former director of Children's Education for the General Conference Mennonite Church, developed the "Creative Movements for Beatitudes."

I am grateful to Kathy Giesbrecht, longtime teacher of junior highs at Burrows Bethel Mennonite Church in Winnipeg, for helping to make this course junior-high friendly.

Living the Beatitudes is an eight-session Bible study curriculum for junior high students that explores what it means to be a follower of Christ.

Printed on recycled paper in the United States of America
97 96 95 94 4 3 2 1
Library of Congress Number 93-74973
International Standard Book Number 0-87303-211-X

Editorial direction for Faith & Life Press by Susan E. Janzen; editing by Eddy Hall; copyediting by Edna Krueger Dyck; design by Jim L. Friesen; printing by Mennonite Press.

TABLE OF CONTENTS

INTRODUCTION

Teachers in Jesus' day had no overhead transparencies, teaching videos, computers, or even books and paper. They had to teach orally. Yet often when Jesus taught he was surrounded by crowds of eager listeners.

What made Jesus' teaching so intriguing?

For one thing, Jesus often told parables, stories designed to dramatize the truths he was teaching. He would also, after telling a story or giving a long teaching, summarize the central truth in a short saying his listeners could easily remember.

The Sermon on the Mount, found in Matthew 5—7, is made up of just such pithy sayings. Not really a single sermon at all, it is rather a collection of the "punch lines" from twenty or so sermons. Jesus' listeners, upon remembering Jesus' line about being "the salt of the earth," for example, would be reminded of the whole teaching that Jesus summarized with that phrase.

The Sermon on the Mount is the single most extensive collection of Jesus' teachings we have, a powerful summary of what it means to be Jesus' follower. These teachings are for Jesus' disciples—those who have already begun to follow him. Obeying these teachings is not optional for those who would be faithful disciples. They are at the heart of what it means to live as Christians.

While these are instructions for believers, those who are not yet Christians, while "listening in," may get a clearer picture of what it means to be a follower of Jesus, and be inspired to follow too.

As junior highs begin to exercise their recently acquired ability to think abstractly, many will be wondering: Why should I follow Jesus? What does God expect of me? How will my life be different if I follow Jesus? The Beatitudes are a great place for them to look for answers to these questions.

By the end of this study your students will understand better what God expects of followers, will have reflected on their own lives in relation to these expectations, and will have been inspired by people whose lives have exemplified the Beatitudes. Some may have become new followers of Jesus and others will have taken specific steps of obedience on their journeys of faith.

FOR FURTHER READING

The Christian Way by John Miller (Scottdale: Herald Press, 1969).

Sermon on the Mount by Clarence Jordan (Valley Forge: Judson Press, 1952).

SESSION 1

"It's Good to Be Poor" uses Matthew 5:3 to help students understand that we can only begin our journey with Jesus when we realize we cannot make it on our own.

SESSION 2

"Say You're Sorry!" based on Matthew 5:4, will show teens how they can ask for and receive forgiveness when they fall short of God's expectations.

SESSION 3

"Macho or Meek?" asks, Does a Christian always have to give in to others? In this lesson from Matthew 5:5, teens will learn that to be meek is to give God control of their lives.

SESSION 4

"What Are You Hungry For?" looks at Matthew 5:6. In this lesson, students will evaluate their motives and be challenged to allow their concerns for fairness and justice motivate their actions.

SESSION 5

"Have Mercy" uses Matthew 5:7 to encourage students to listen more attentively to others and respond to hurting people with active compassion.

SESSION 6

"How's Your Heart Condition?" based on Matthew 5:8, looks at the motives behind our actions.

SESSION 7

"Me, a Peacemaker?" builds on Matthew 5:9 to empower teens to be peacemakers in a world that increasingly encourages the use of violence to solve problems.

SESSION 8

"Why Do Good If It Gets Me Into Trouble?" examines why standing up for what is right sometimes gets us into trouble. Students will be challenged by Matthew 5:10 to do the right thing in the face of pressures to compromise.

HOW TO TEACH THIS COURSE

From Life to Bible to Life

The teaching plan used in this study is called life-centered because our teaching begins with a life situation. After discussing a common situation teens may experience, we search the Scriptures to see what God has to say about the issue. Then we return to the life situation and consider practical applications and age-appropriate responses to the situation.

The Bible is at the center of this study both literally and methodologically. Since we feel the Bible ought to speak to every life issue, it is central to the studies that follow.

USING THE TEACHER'S GUIDE

PREPARATION

Orient yourself to the lesson by reading through the Preparation section. Here you will find the central focus of the lesson as well as the teaching objective.

Scripture text

The session is rooted in this Bible passage. Read through it to gain a sense of what the text is saying. What strikes you as you read it?

Key verse

This verse summarizes the Scripture passage.

Faith focus

This is the story of the Scripture passage in a nutshell. Here is the nugget of truth on which we will focus this lesson.

Session goal

As you teach, be aware of your goal. What outcomes of this lesson—changes in knowledge, attitude, or action—do you desire in your students?

Materials needed and advance preparation

You will find a list of what you will need to carry

through the suggested lesson plan. Glance over this part a week before you teach this lesson.

EXPLORATION

Carefully follow the five step-by-step movements through the lesson. They will carry you from life to the Bible and back to life. The variety of activities should appeal to different kinds of learners and keep your students from getting bored.

1. Focus. This movement serves two purposes: to create a friendly climate in the classroom and to focus attention on the session's topic. Usually this beginning step will be interactive and fun.

2. Connect. Here the student's experience is connected to the issue. In a variety of ways, students are drawn in to share their experiences as they relate to this topic.

3. Hear and enter. Attention turns to the Bible passage. Students are invited to enter into dialogue with the faith story and explore what it has to say to the questions raised by the issue in the earlier steps. The emphasis is to help students discover new insights into the Scriptures.

4. Apply. "So what?" is the question discussed here. How does the Scripture relate to and apply to the issue under consideration?

5. Respond. What are the students willing to do as a result of their study? How will their attitudes and actions be different as a result of this study?

REFLECT AND LOOK AHEAD

Evaluative questions help you reflect on the experience of this session. Here are also reminders of what you need to do for the next session.

DIGGING DEEPER

This section provides background and insights for step 3 through additional comments and interpretations of the Scripture text. Read it and let it inspire your teaching.

STUDENT HANDOUT

Each session includes activity handouts that may be photocopied and distributed to the students.

JUNIOR HIGH IS NOT A DISEASE!

Just like adults, junior high youth have their good days and bad days, their ups and downs, and experience a range of feelings and emotions.

Sometimes they feel lonely, frustrated, insecure, moody, happy, anxious, relaxed, confused, determined, and driven.

Sometimes they are bored, competent, capable, delighted, quarrelsome, caring, helpful, indifferent, cautious, optimistic, discouraged, proud, and remorseful. Adults are all those things, too.

WHO ARE JUNIOR HIGHS?

Developmentally there are some significant differences between young teens and adults:

- Young teens are just beginning to learn to think and reason abstractly.
- Their attention span ranges from four to seven minutes.
- If it takes you more than 1.2 seconds to change activities, you will lose them.
- They are a visual generation. Pictures have replaced words.
- They are active and energetic. Learning must be activity oriented.
- They are an image generation. They hate to be singled out, made to look stupid, or appear "uncool." They respond well to positive reinforcement.
- They respond in half the time that it takes adults to respond.

Other tips junior high leaders might find helpful:

- Overplan so you do not run out of ideas.
- Develop a "quiet box" with various noisemakers you might use to get their attention.
- Do activities that build up kids' self-esteem rather than forcing them to compete or stand alone.

LEARNING STYLES [1]

Each of us has a special way in which we process or use what we see. This is called our learning style. We learn best when we are taught in ways that complement our learning style.

Where do learning styles come from? Our heredity, past life experiences, the style of a favorite teacher, and the demands of our environment all help create our learning style.

Recent research has shown that there are four main learning styles among North Americans:

- Innovative learners—people who learn by small group interaction and role playing.
- Analytic learners—people who learn through stories and demonstrations.
- Common sense learners—people who learn by doing.
- Dynamic learners—people who learn by creating.

Effective leaders keep in mind that what is comfortable for them as teachers might not be best for those whose learning styles differ from theirs. No style is right or wrong. We simply learn in different ways. Try to plan at least one activity per session for learners in each of these styles.

1 The section on learning styles draws from the work of Marlene LeFever in *Creative Teaching Methods* (D.C. Cook, 1985).

SESSION 1: IT'S GOOD TO BE POOR

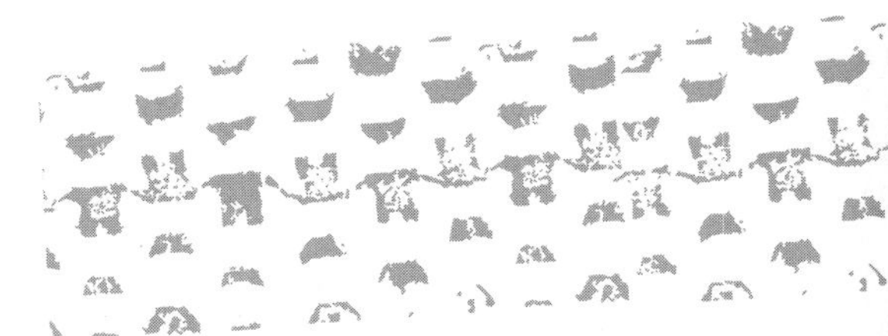

PREPARATION

Key verse: Blessed are the poor in spirit, for theirs is the kingdom of heaven. (Matthew 5:3)

Faith focus: The first step of our journey into the kingdom of God is realizing that we cannot go it alone without God.

Session goal: Help students recognize or reaffirm the reality that they are not equal to life's demands without God.

Materials needed and advance preparation:
- A combination lock (Focus, Option 2).
- Bibles.
- Copy handouts (Connect, Option 1; Respond).
- Learn actions for the first Beatitude if using them for Hear and Enter.
- Index cards, if you choose to use them for Hear and Enter.

EXPLORATION

Words intended to be spoken to the class are printed in italics.

FOCUS
(4-8 minutes)

Option 1: Say: *All your life you've heard about this wonderful beach in Manitoba, Canada. Finally you are old enough to drive and you and your best friend set out in your parents' old station wagon to find this beach. You have a map that shows you how to get to Manitoba, but after that you're not sure which roads to take. As soon as you cross the border, you ask a service station attendant. She tells you to go forty-five miles north and sixteen miles west and then follow the signs. After traveling thirty-three miles north, you come to road construction and have to take an alternate route. You become thoroughly lost. Another person your age comes along and you ask him how to get to the beach. "Just follow me," he says. "I'm on my way there right now."*

After forty-five minutes on winding roads, you get to the

beach. It's just as wonderful as you were told and you have a great weekend there.

List everything you did that made it possible for you to get to the beach. Here are some possible answers:.

- had a destination in mind
- had a vehicle to get there
- went with a friend
- used a map
- asked attendant for directions
- followed a guide

Option 2: Bring a combination lock to the meeting. As teens arrive, ask them to find the combination that opens it. As an incentive, you could say that anyone who opens it can keep the lock or receive a food prize. When everyone has tried to open it, show how easily it opens with the right combination.

CONNECT
(4-8 minutes)

If you used Option 1: Pass out copies of the handout, "Tips for a Good Trip." Drawing on the previous activity, have students fill in the road signs with travel tips and instructions for the journey of life. (For example, know where you are going, travel with others, ask for help when lost, use a map, follow a guide.) Once they've used up the ideas growing out of the previous activity, have them make up tips of their own, either lighthearted or serious.

If you used Option 2, say: Trying to open that lock without the right combination must have been frustrating. Can you think of other times when you felt frustrated and helpless? Ask the students to describe those situations. They might include when:

- their parents grounded them after their report card marks came in too low
- they arm wrestled someone bigger than themselves
- they couldn't remember the math formula they knew until they began the test
- they saw a house on fire but couldn't save what was inside
- they were tobogganing down a hill and couldn't control the direction

Discuss: *What can you do when you face an impossible situation?*

Transition comment: *If you used Option 1, say: In some ways the Christian life is like an trip. Our goal or destination is loving God and others, the Bible is our map, the traveling companions are other Christians, and our guide is God's Spirit. The Beatitudes are part of Jesus' teachings and therefore guide us toward our destination.*

If you used Option 2, say: *Sooner or later we all face situations in life that are beyond our control, problems we can't overcome on our own. As frustrating as these times are, they present us with the opportunity to learn one of the most valuable truths we can ever learn.*

HEAR AND ENTER
(10-15 minutes)

Part 1: At the back of this book are suggested actions to go with each Beatitude. If you think your group would enjoy using these, learn the actions and teach your group the first Beatitude using words and actions together.

Another memory method is to write each word of Matthew 5:3 on a separate index card. Have the students gather around a table or a bare spot on the floor. Shuffle the cards and pass them out to students. Time the group to see how long it takes them to arrange the words of the verse in the correct order. Repeat this once or twice to see if they can break their own record (and to reinforce the memorization of the verse).

Still another approach is to go around the group having the first teen say the first word of the verse, the second teen saying the second word, and so on through the end of the verse. This can be repeated starting with a different person. A variation is to have each student say two words of the verse, or three, before going on to the next student. After you think most of the students know the verse, have the class say the whole verse in unison. Then call on individual students to say it.

Part 2: Ask for a volunteer to be the "roving reporter." (If no one volunteers, you can be the reporter.) Use one or both of the following Bible stories, depending on the size of your group and the amount of time you have. If you use only one story, ask the entire class to read the story silently. Tell them they are bystanders who just witnessed the story they read. The roving reporter will interview them to find out what happened. If two stories are used, divide into two groups and assign each group a different story to read.

Possible questions to ask: *What happened? What do you think about it?* (Follow up on any comments that mention that a person in leadership humbled himself to ask for Jesus' help.) *What do you think about Jesus? Do you think Jesus could help you?*

Bible stories to use: Matthew 8:5-13; Matthew 9:18-26.

APPLY
(10-15 minutes)

Option 1: Tell the group about a time in your own life when you realized you needed to depend on God or others.

For example, I remember flying in an airplane when there was some turbulence and the oxygen masks dropped down for us to use. During the next five minutes, I thought we were going to crash, and there was nothing I could do about it. My life was literally in God's hands.

During the early years of our marriage, my wife and I owned only one car. My wife was a nurse and occasionally worked on Sundays. I often had to ask church friends who lived nearby for a ride to and from church. I hated asking for a ride because I felt so dependent. However, I found I enjoyed their company and soon we became better friends because we rode together.

After sharing one or two similar incidents from your life, invite some of your students to do the same. Say, *It seems that our affluence makes us feel less dependent on God and others. Is that good or bad? Should we keep ourselves poor so we'll be more dependent on God?*

Option 2: Organize a debate by dividing your class into two groups. From the following list, select two or three statements that will interest your group. For the first statement ask group A to debate in support of the statement and group B to oppose it. For the next statement have B debate in support of the statement and A against, and so on.

Propositions for debate

- As long as there are exams in the classroom, there will be prayer in schools.
- People can live without God and still be happy.
- If you really trust God, you will never question God.
- If God had never given us the Bible, people would have figured out how to live anyway.
- If you trust God, everything will work out for you.

Option 3: The following story tells of a person who was "poor in spirit." Read it to the class.

Corrie ten Boom was born in Haarlem, Holland, to a wealthy watchmaker in the 1890s. She had always been brought up with a deep faith in God. She believed that if there was a tough situation and you trusted God, he would not necessarily zap it away, but would help you cope with it.

Corrie's family had always been very hospitable. When World War II broke out, her family began taking in Jewish families who were hiding or fleeing. In the ten Boom's house was a secret room where they hid the refugees. One day the ten Booms were betrayed by a spy posing as a Jew. They were handed over to the authorities and sent to a concentration camp. Corrie's father and sister died there. Corrie trusted that God would do what was best, and that meant she would be released or she too would die.

Her life was spared. When she later wrote about her life, she wrote about it not as though it was her work, but rather God's work which she had been able to do through faith in God. During her time in prison, she learned to depend on God and recognize the important role God played in her daily life. (Story by Jeremy)

RESPOND
(5-10 minutes)

Option 1: Pass out the "Faith Hero" handout. Ask each teen to think of a person who exemplifies Matthew 5:3. The person may be a relative, someone they know in the congregation, even someone who has died. When most are done, invite several students to read their stories to the class.

Option 2: Pass out the "Faith Hero" handout. Ask teens to place X's on the two continuums, then to write out a three-step action plan for how to move from where they are to where they want to be in trusting God.

Next have them form pairs to share their responses. Based on the sharing, ask partners to pray for one another, either aloud or in silence.

REFLECT AND LOOK AHEAD

In this study we want to encourage the students to see the Christian life as a journey consisting of many steps. Have students come away from this lesson with one specific faith step they can take. Do they sense their need for God because of their inadequacy to face life's challenges alone?

DIGGING DEEPER

The first step in following Jesus is to realize that we need him—that we cannot make it on our own. People who are very poor materially realize that they have to depend on others for their needs. Until we recognize our spiritual poverty, we won't realize how much we need God.

Most of us live most of the time as though we don't need God. When things go well for us, we may feel like we are in control and can handle whatever comes. But when circumstances bring us face-to-face with our limitations—when tragedy strikes, when we need strength to confront a difficult situation, or when a friend betrays us, our illusion of self-sufficiency is broken. In these moments, God's grace tries to break in, inviting us to depend on God. It is to those who let go of their illusions of self-sufficiency and embrace God's sufficiency that the kingdom of heaven belongs.

Some of the junior highs in your group may not yet be on the Christian journey. You may want to spend time with individuals or the whole class talking about becoming followers of Jesus. Share why you have chosen to be on this journey.

HANDOUTS

Tips for a Good Trip
Faith Hero

Tips for a Good Trip

If life was a trip along a road, what travel tips do you think should appear on signs along the way?

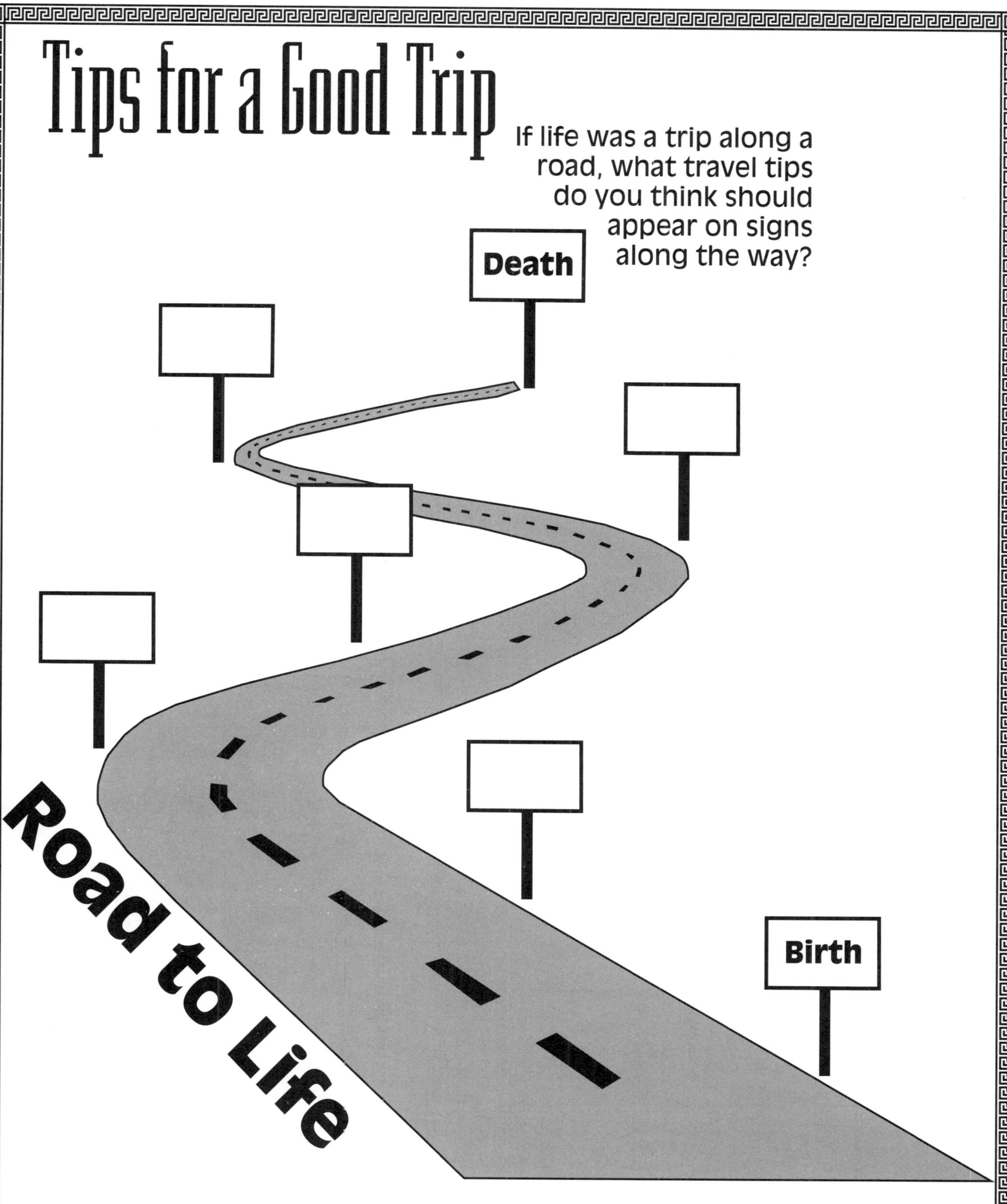

Faith Hero

A person I know who depends (or depended) on God like Corrie ten Boom did is

______________________________________.

Briefly write this person's story.

Place yourself (X) somewhere on this line.

I have learned to trust God fully — I struggle to trust God

Now put an X where you would like to be.

I have learned to trust God fully — I struggle to trust God

What would you need to do to move closer to your goal? Write an action plan that will help you do that.

Step 1

Step 2

Step 3

SESSION 2:

SAY YOU'RE SORRY!

PREPARATION

Key verse: Blessed are those who mourn, for they will be comforted. (Matthew 5:4)

Faith focus: By repenting of our failures, we can receive forgiveness and make a new start.

Session goal: Encourage students to ask for and receive forgiveness from God and others when they have done wrong.

Materials needed and advance preparation:

- A sculpted figure made of play dough (Focus, Option 1).
- Bibles.
- Index cards and pencils (Connect, Option 2).
- Chalkboard, or newsprint and marker.
- Colored markers, pencils, and scissors (Respond, optional)
- If you are using the actions with the Beatitudes, review those for the first Beatitude and learn those for the second.
- Make copies of handouts (Apply, Option 1; Respond, optional).

EXPLORATION

FOCUS
(2-4 minutes)

Option 1: Make a little human figure from play dough or plasticine and name him Cleapas. Give him a cute button nose, spaghetti hair, and a goofy smile. Tell your students the following story: *I'd like to introduce you to Cleapas. I spent a long time creating him and am really proud of my work. Maybe I'll enter him in the county fair this summer. The other day I brought him to church. You will never believe what happened. I set him down on the coat rack along with some books and went to the washroom. When I came back, I couldn't find him. What do you think happened to him?* (Someone stole him, someone moved him.)

I looked around and found him on the floor. No, he hadn't fallen. Someone had deliberately thrown him on the floor, stepped on him, and flattened him. (If you want to be dramatic, flatten him with your fist.) *How do you think I felt when I saw him?* (Angry, sad, discouraged, resentful, unhappy.)

Option 2: Read the following story to your group:
Jana and Karen were best friends. Jana invited Karen to join their family for a camping trip for four days. The campground where they stayed showed films every evening from 9:00 until 10:00. Since there was little else to do at that hour they decided to go. They found the films boring, though, so they decided to leave. Just outside the theater they met some guys. They decided to go for a walk together since they were not expected to be home until 10:30. At 11:30, Jana's parents got worried about them and began looking for them and got the park rangers to help them look. At midnight the girls came walking casually into the campsite. They couldn't understand why everyone was so upset. After all, they had just been out walking on a lovely night.

Discuss:

- *How do you think Jana and Karen felt?*
- *Did Jana and Karen do anything wrong?*
- *If you were Jana's parents, what would you do?*
- *What consequences should there be for Jana and Karen?*

(This really happened. Jana's parents made them write an apology to the rangers. They ended the camping trip and went home early the next morning. Jana and Karen felt Jana's parents made too big a deal of what happened. What do you think?)

CONNECT
(3-6 minutes)

If you used Option 1 above, ask: *What would make me feel better after the untimely demise of Cleapas?* Possible answers:

- finding out who did it and destroying something he or she created
- recreating him
- getting an apology from the person who destroyed him

Discuss: *Try to agree on a consequence for the person who destroyed Cleapas.*

If you used Option 2 above, hand out index cards and ask your teens to write down the worst thing they ever got in trouble for. Collect the cards and read them anonymously to the class. After each situation, ask how this person might have felt.

Discuss: *What should have been a consequence of this action?*

Transition comment: *It's impossible to go through a week or even a day without offending someone or doing something wrong. Sometimes people get really upset with us. At other times it seems like they don't care. When we do something that offends others, our relationship with them becomes strained. But if we are sorry for the things we do that hurt others and God, we will be blessed by God's forgiveness and comfort.*

HEAR AND ENTER

(10-15 minutes)

Part 1: Teach your group the second Beatitude, Matthew 5:4. Review the first Beatitude and put the two together until the entire group can recite them. Use any of the memorization methods described in Session 1 (Hear and Enter), with or without the actions shown at the back of this book.

Part 2: Explain: *The second step in following Jesus is to "mourn," to be sorry for the wrongs we do. The good news is that when we do something wrong, we can be forgiven if we admit our sin and ask for forgiveness. Asking forgiveness takes courage. Here is a story about a person who mourned and had the courage to change his ways.*

Read or ask one of the students to read the following story:

Charles Colson was tough. As a former navy officer he learned about the corrupt U.S. political system. Being one of its best players, he rose in its ranks. In 1972 he was a high ranking officer in the executive branch of government under President Nixon.

In 1973 after involvement in the Watergate scandal, Colson was sentenced to a maximum of three years in prison.

He always thought he knew about laws and the legal system. In jail he learned of its victims and did much to help them. During the indictment hearings, he learned about and accepted Jesus as his Savior. For his sins and naivete he mourned and was "born again." (Story by Jeremy)

Discuss:

- *Can you think of any situation where you might not be able to forgive someone?*
- *One definition of sin is "any thought or action that harms me or my neighbor, now or in the future." What do you think of that definition? Would you add anything to it?*

Part 3: Prepare for the reading of John 8:1-11 by having your class portray two or three "still life" scenes from the story. Depending on the size of your group, divide the class into two or three groups. Assign verses 1-5 to the first group, 6-8 to the second group, and 9-11 to the third group. Each group is to get into a "freeze" position that captures the scene of the passage. For example, the first group could have a woman in the middle with several standing around her, pointing fingers at her.

When the groups have had enough time to prepare their scene, bring the groups together. Have one group at a time create its scene. While they stay "frozen," read the verses they are portraying.

Note: While the passage does not say that the woman was sorry for what she had done, the forgiveness Jesus extended and his command, "Go and sin no more," implies an attitude of repentance.

APPLY
(10-15 minutes)

Option 1: Sometimes we need courage or encouragement to say we are sorry. At other times we need help in knowing how best to say we are sorry. Write the following four steps on the chalkboard:

a) Look directly at the person to whom you want to say "I'm sorry."
b) Tell specifically what you are sorry about. Say, "I'm sorry that I..."
c) Make a follow-up statement. Either, "Is there any way I can make it up to you?" or "It won't happen again."
d) Thank the person for listening.

Have students practice the four steps by using the situations described in the handout, "Learning to Say 'I'm Sorry.'"

Option 2: Discuss:

a) *What happens when we don't seek forgiveness?* (keeps us apart from others, creates distance, makes true friendship impossible)
b) *When someone is wronged, whose responsibility is it to make things right?* (usually the person who has wronged someone, but sometimes a person may not be aware that he or she has offended someone, then it is that person's responsibility to say how they have been wronged)
c) *Brainstorm ideas that would give a person courage to*

deal with an unforgiven issue. (prayer, talking to a friend, hearing a sermon, reading Scripture)

Option 3: Debate the following statement: *It is enough to ask God for forgiveness; I don't need to ask forgiveness from the person I have wronged.*

RESPOND
(5-10 minutes)

List the four A's of forgiveness on a chalkboard or newsprint.

The Four A's of Forgiveness

ACKNOWLEDGE to yourself that you offended someone.
ADMIT the specific thing you did to the person you offended, and commit not to do it again.
ASK what you can do to make it right.
ACCEPT the person's forgiveness.

Have students form pairs and talk about which step they find the most difficult.

Optional: Using the "Forgiveness Bookmark" handout, have students create bookmarks as reminders of the four steps of forgiveness (instructions on handout). Make scissors and colored markers available.

Closing prayer: Invite each group member to think of a past deed he or she is truly sorry for. If they have not already done so, encourage them to confess what they did to God. If it has resulted in someone being wronged, ask God to help him or her know how best to deal with that situation in the near future.

REFLECT AND LOOK AHEAD

This second step on the journey is one we have to take many times because we frequently fail others. It takes courage and humility to admit to others that we wronged them. Yet often a sincere "I'm sorry" will go a long way.

Did your group come away with a sense of the importance of "mourning" for their sins? Will they have the tools and encouragement they need to deal with the sin in their lives?

DIGGING DEEPER

Charles Colson is an example of someone who was sorry about the direction his life was going and decided that he wanted to journey with Jesus. Maybe there are teens in your group who are unhappy with their present life and want to change direction. Invite such students to talk to you individually outside of the group meetings.

HANDOUTS

Learning to Say "I'm Sorry"
Forgiveness Bookmark

Learning to Say "I'm Sorry"

Form groups of three. Decide who will be person A, B, and C. For the first situation, person A asks B for forgiveness. Person C observes whether the four-step process was followed. If any of the steps is left out, Person C suggests how it might have been included. Then B asks C for forgiveness and A observes and so on.

Situation 1: You spread a nasty rumor that you saw ______ and ________ making out in the student lounge after school yesterday.

Situation 3: You are jealous that Kiera received a higher mark in science than you did, so you called her a geek.

Situation 2: You told your parents you were going to be at your best friend's house all evening when instead the two of you went to hang out at the mall.

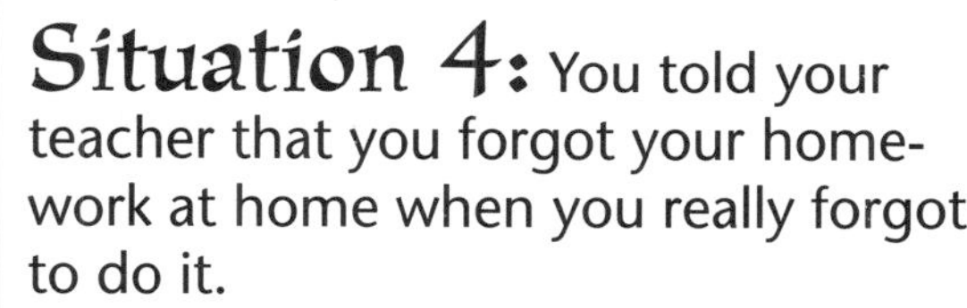

Situation 4: You told your teacher that you forgot your homework at home when you really forgot to do it.

Situation 5: You feel guilty about the trashy movie you rented.

Situation 6: You walked out of the music store with a music tape you didn't pay for.

Forgiveness Bookmark

In the space below, design a bookmark that will help you remember the four A's of forgiveness:

•Acknowledge •Admit •Ask •Accept

On the back side, write in pencil the name of a person from whom you want to seek forgiveness. Once you have asked the person's forgiveness, erase his or her name.

Forgiveness Bookmark

In the space below, design a bookmark that will help you remember the four A's of forgiveness:

•Acknowledge •Admit •Ask •Accept

On the back side, write in pencil the name of a person from whom you want to seek forgiveness. Once you have asked the person's forgiveness, erase his or her name.

Copyright © 1994 by Faith & Life Press. Permission is granted to photocopy this handout for use with Session 2 (RESPOND, Optional Activity).

SESSION 3: MACHO OR MEEK?

PREPARATION

Key verse: Blessed are the meek, for they will inherit the earth. (Matthew 5:5)

Faith focus: Jesus calls us to be meek—submitted to God's will and dependent on God's power. It is the meek, not the aggressive and domineering, who will inherit the earth.

Session goal: Help teens see through the cool, tough, in control images that are held up for admiration in our culture, and encourage them to seek to be meek—submitted to God's will and dependent on God's power.

Materials needed and advance preparation:

- Chalkboard or newsprint and marker (Connect, Option 2).
- Pencils.
- If you are using the actions with the Beatitudes, learn those for Matthew 5:5.
- Make copies of the drama of Moses and recruit four students to read it in class (Hear and Enter, Option 1).
- Rope (Apply, Option 2).
- Make copies of the handout (Respond, Option 2)
- Fill out for yourself the self-inventory on the handout, "How Meek Are You?"

EXPLORATION

FOCUS
(3-5 minutes)

Begin the class by playing "Simon says...." For those who have forgotten the rules, the leader makes a statement and does the action at the same time. If the statement begins with "Simon says" then everyone must follow the stated action. If the leader says, "do a jumping jack" but does not begin the command with "Simon says," then the group should not do the action. Those who are tricked into following the command that does not begin with "Simon says" are considered out. The last one "in" becomes Simon.

Play until several from the class have had a turn at being Simon.

CONNECT
(3-5 minutes)

Option 1: Ask everyone to find a partner and give the pairs two minutes to develop a thirty-second skit illustrating what it means to be meek. After every pair has presented a picture of meekness, have them describe the kind of words that came to mind during the skits. Some words that they might use are: *wimp, quiet, sissy, someone who doesn't fight back, calm, patient.*

Option 2: Draw a sketch of "Meek Mary" on the chalkboard. Ask the class to list some characteristics of a meek person. Jot these on the chalkboard (*gentle, quiet, submissive, sensitive, docile, delicate*).

Transition comment: *When we think of meek, the pictures that come into our minds are quite different than the picture that Jesus had in mind when he called the meek blessed. Jesus' idea of meek can be illustrated by the simple game "Simon says." In this game, you win by obeying only the commands that Simon gives. In life we win by obeying God's commands. When we give ourselves to God's will and trust God for what we need, we become meek. Let's explore further what the Bible teaches us about being meek.*

HEAR AND ENTER
(15-20 minutes)

Part 1: Use the method of your choice to teach the class Matthew 5:5. As a group, practice reciting the first three Beatitudes together, with or without the accompanying actions, until the entire class can recite them. Use any of the memorization methods described in Session 1 (Hear and Enter) that work best for your class.

Part 2: Option 1: Invite four students to read the drama of Moses. Discuss: *How did Moses change between Scene 1 and Scene 2? What brought about this difference?*

Part 2: Option 2: As a class, try to tell the story of Moses from memory. Then ask them to identify times when Moses did and did not exhibit "meekness"—i.e., did not allow God to control his life and depend on God's power and guidance.

Be prepared to guide the group in interpreting Moses' life in the following way. *Say, Moses was transformed from being an angry, impulsive young man who tried without success to save his people in his own strength to a powerful leader who no longer depended on his own power but God's. What do you think* brought about this *transformation? Do you think Moses could have led his people to freedom if he had continued to try to be in control?* (Some of this happened during the time he was mentored by his father-in-law, Jethro, and some happened when he spent time with God while herding sheep in the wilderness.)

APPLY
(8-12 minutes)

Part 1: Review what Jesus means by *meek* when he says, "Blessed are the meek." Come of up with a definition of *meek* the class can agree on. Begin by asking them to use phrases that describe Moses. Then try to compose a definition that summarizes the suggestions. (For example, "To be meek is to submit to God's will and depend on God's power.")

Part 2: Option 1: As a class think of one or two people who are "meek" in the biblical sense. These may be people in your church or community. Ask students why they consider these people meek. Do they admire them? want to be like them? Why or why not?

Part 2: Option 2: For this object lesson, you will need to bring a rope or string to class. It should reach about two-thirds of the way across the room. Place the rope on the floor and stretch it as far as it will go, keeping one end close to the wall.

Ask a volunteer to begin at the wall and walk along the rope to the opposite wall in the room. Every step taken must be along the rope. When he or she gets to the end of the rope, ask the class to suggest ways that the volunteer can finish crossing the room without the volunteer using his or her hands to move the rope. (Answer: Someone from class could move the rope which has already been walked on around the volunteer and stretch it to the wall so the walk can be completed.)

Say: The object lesson illustrates that in life we often need the help of others (and God) to accomplish our goals. However, frequently we look to God only when we come to the end of our rope. God is there for us at that time, but wants us to depend on him at all times, not only when we are stuck and have no other options.

RESPOND
(5-10 minutes)

Hand out copies of the self-inventory, "How Meek Are You?" Be sure you have filled this out for yourself before class. Read or explain the instructions at the top of the handout, then give the students two or three minutes to fill out their inventories.

Closing Prayer: Invite students to pray for those sitting on their left, asking God to bless them as they seek to trust God with control of their lives.

REFLECT AND LOOK AHEAD

The concept of meekness may be difficult to get across to junior highs. Some would rather be cool, tough, self-sufficient, or in control than to let God control their lives. If they can come to see dependence on God as something positive, they can gain freedom from the pressure of having to go it alone and can take part in God's purpose in the world.

DIGGING DEEPER

The picture of meekness that first comes to mind is not a very attractive one. Usually we equate meek with being a wimp. That is not what the Bible means by meek. If we want to challenge teens to be meek, we'll need to show them it doesn't mean wimpiness.

A meek person is one who submits to God's will. This does not mean that the meek person has no ideas or plans, but he or she evaluates those plans in light of God's will to see if they are God's plans. If not, the meek person changes those plans.

The meek person is one who depends on God's power. He or she knows that in human power it is impossible to do God's will. God's work and God's will can only be accomplished by God's power.

Matthew uses the term *meek* to refer to the way Jesus exercised his authority. There was nothing wimpish about the way he challenged the Pharisees and went about preaching to the crowds. He was active, not passive. Because he was in tune with God's will, he could proceed with confidence and proper timing.

Moses is also described as meek (or sometimes translated *humble*). In Numbers 12:3 we read, "Now Moses was a very humble man, more humble than anyone else on the face of the earth" (NIV). Moses was one of the greatest leaders in the Old Testament—certainly no spineless character. What made him great? His obedience to God's will.

Someone has observed that Moses' life can be summarized as follows: The first forty years Moses tried to become a somebody. For the next forty years he became a nobody. During the last forty years he showed what God could do with a nobody. During the second period of his life, while tending sheep, he came to know God's will for his life, then carried it out during his last forty years.

HANDOUTS

Moses
How Meek Are You?

M O S E S

A drama by John W. Miller

Cast
Moses, about forty years old in Scene 1, older in Scene 2.
Jethro, fifty or more years old
Zipporah, who becomes Moses' wife after Scene 1
Gershom, ten-year-old son of Moses and Zipporah

Scene 1

Zipporah: Father, Father!

Jethro [*offstage*]: Yes? What is it? I'm over here.

Zipporah [*turning in direction of voice*]: Father, a man...a stranger!

Jethro [*coming onstage*]: Why Zipporah, you're home early today. Is everything all right?

Zipporah [*trying to calm down*]: We were at the well, Father, just beginning to draw water for the sheep, when the shepherds of Lamech arrived with their flocks.

Jethro [*stern*]: Did they push you away again!

Zipporah: Yes, Father, as they always do!

Jethro: This has got to stop. I must talk to Lamech. Surely he knows what his shepherds are doing. Has he no respect for my daughters?

Zipporah: But, Father, today a stranger helped us.

Jethro: That's why you're home so early then!

Zipporah: Yes, this is what I'm trying to tell you. They were chasing us away when suddenly there was this man, beating them away with his stick. They were as surprised as we were, and didn't lift a finger against him. Then he drew water for our sheep until they were all watered (Exod. 2:15 ff.).

Jethro: Where did this stranger come from?

Zipporah: He's an Egyptian!

Jethro: An Egyptian! Then what's he doing in the wilderness of Midian? He must be in trouble. Where is he?

Zipporah [*pointing*]: There, with the sheep.

Jethro [*turning and calling in direction of Moses*]: Shalom! You are welcome to the tents of Jethro.

Moses [*coming onstage, bowing low as he approaches Jethro*]: Shalom, my lord. You are most gracious to a stranger.

Jethro: My daughter tells me that you have been of great help in watering the sheep.

Moses [*standing tall, flashing a bit of anger*]: It disturbs me, sir, to see anyone being mistreated. And your daughters were being badly mistreated.

Jethro: Yes, and there's not much I can do about it. I have no sons. [*pause*] What is your name? And where do you come from?

Moses: Moses, sir. I grew up in the household of Pharaoh but my people are the Hebrews who work there as slaves.

Jethro: Ah, yes. They are badly treated, we hear.
Moses [*again with a flash of anger*]: What you have heard is true!
Jethro: How is it then that you lived in Pharaoh's household?
Moses: That, sir, is a long story...but I never forgot my people [*flashing anger*], and I never will.
Jethro: Then what brings you to the wilderness of Midian?
Moses: I seek refuge, sir, and time to think. Time to discover what I can do to help my people.
Jethro: Refuge? Have you done something wrong, Moses?
Moses: No, sir! I murdered an Egyptian who beat a Hebrew slave (Exod. 2:11). Yes, I murdered him. But I have done nothing wrong.
Jethro: Ah, yes...you take the side of your people. I can see that. What god do you serve, Moses?
Moses: None, sir.
Jethro: You worship no god?
Moses: In Pharaoh's household I was taught to worship Pharaoh himself, and the sun-god, Atum-Re. Among my people I learned of the God of my fathers, the God of Abraham.
Jethro: And you serve none of these gods?
Moses [*angry*]: If the God of my fathers is God, why should I? What has he done for my people? And if Pharaoh is god, why is he so cruel? Even if it were true that he is god, I would never worship him.
Jethro [*coming to Moses, placing an arm on his shoulder*]: Stay with us, Moses. I lack a shepherd for my flocks, a husband for my eldest daughter. [*At this statement Zipporah gasps audibly, turns in embarrassment and exits, hands to face.*] You lack a god. Perhaps we can be of help to one another. What do you say?
Moses: Thank you, sir. You are very kind. I will accept your offer.
Jethro: Then go, wash from your journey and join us for the evening meal. Zipporah, tell the servants to make ready a tent for Moses. [*Turning, he notices that Zipporah is no longer there.*] Zipporah!? Well, where did she go? Come, Moses, I'll take you myself. [*They begin to exit.*] You'll be a great help to us.

Scene 2
Many years later. Moses returns home after months of herding sheep in distant pastures.

[*A horn blasts offstage. Then voices are heard shouting:* Moses! Look! Moses! It's Moses!]
Zipporah [*running onstage, with Gershom*]: It's Moses! Gershom, see, it's your father! Oh thank God. [*They watch intently toward stage front.*]
Jethro [*walking slowly onstage, standing slightly to the rear of Zipporah and Gershom*]: It's good to see him again. I miss him when he's gone—almost as much as you do, Zipporah, I think.
Zipporah: See how he walks, Father.
Jethro: What do you mean?
Zipporah: Much stronger. And his head!
Jethro: Yes, he holds it higher.
Zipporah [*turning now full face to Jethro*]: Father, do you think...?
Jethro: We must not stand in his way, Zipporah.
Zipporah: But what if...
Jethro: Don't be afraid, my daughter.
Zipporah [*turning around suddenly, facing Moses as he approaches*]: Moses!
Moses [*coming down center aisle and onto stage, greets Zipporah, turns to Gershom*]: Zipporah! Gershom! Jethro! [*embraces them*] God be praised!
Jethro: God has prospered your journey, Moses?

Moses: Beyond my expectations!
Gershom: Did you see any lions, Father?
Moses: No, Gershom, but many snakes.
Zipporah: Oh, it's so good to have you safely back home.
Moses: But I'll not be staying, Zipporah.
Zipporah: What?
Moses: Jethro, I must speak at once of what has happened. I have served you now for many years.
Jethro: Why, yes, you have. What is it?
Moses: The time has come for me to go back to Egypt, to learn firsthand how it is with my people there (Exod. 4:18 ff.).
Jethro: Then God has spoken to you?
Moses: Yes! Zipporah, you and Gershom and I, we are going to make this journey together.
Zipporah: Oh, Moses, you frighten me.
Moses: I understand, Zipporah. The thought of it still frightens me, but I must tell you what happened at the mountain of God. Yahweh spoke to me!
Zipporah: Yahweh! Father! Your God! Our God!
Moses: The God of my ancestors.
Jethro: Of Abraham and Sarah, Isaac and Rebekah, and Jacob and Leah and Rachel?
Moses: Yes, Jethro, your God and our God! And he has promised to deliver my people out of their bondage.
Jethro: Then he's stronger and greater than the gods of Egypt?
Moses: Yes, Jethro. Do I have your permission?
Jethro: To leave my tents and return to Egypt?
Moses: Yes.
Jethro [*coming to Moses and putting hands on shoulders*]: Not only my permission, Moses—my blessing! [*They begin to exit.*] But whether Yahweh, the God of my ancestors and of your ancestors, is greater than the gods of Egypt...?
Moses [*to Gershom, taking his hand*]: Come, Gershom, we must get ready for a long journey.
Jethro:...whether God is greater than the sun-god, Atum-Re...
Moses: Zipporah, we shall leave tomorrow if at all possible.
Jethro [*now almost offstage*]:...or greater than Horus the falcon-god—this, Moses, I do not know.
Moses: Then you shall know it, Jethro, and very soon.

How Meek Are You?

Each of the sentences below describes an aspect of meekness as Jesus used the word. Use this inventory to see how far along you are in becoming the kind of person Jesus calls blessed in Matthew 5:5. Circle the number closest to how you feel about yourself.

5 means the statement is true about you most of the time
3 means it is true sometimes
1 means it is never true.

5 4 3 2 1 1. I consciously try to let God control my life.

5 4 3 2 1 2. I depend on God even when I am not at the end of my rope.

5 4 3 2 1 3. I spend time thinking about what God wants me to do with my life.

5 4 3 2 1 4. I try to do what pleases God.

5 4 3 2 1 5. When I am unsure about a decision, I pray about it or seek advice from Christians I trust.

5 4 3 2 1 6. When I clearly know God's will, I am willing to obey.

5 4 3 2 1 7. I realize I can't do God's will or God's work in my own human strength, but that I need to rely on God's power.

After completing this inventory, a goal I have is ____________________

____

____

____

SESSION 4:

WHAT ARE YOU HUNGRY FOR?

PREPARATION

Key verse: Blessed are those who hunger and thirst for righteousness, for they will be filled. (Matthew 5:6)

Faith focus: God calls us to be people with a passionate desire for justice.

Session goal: Challenge teens to desire and work for a more fair and just world.

Materials needed and advance preparation:

- A snack food such as cheese, potato chips, or chocolate.
- A drink, such as cola or chocolate milk, and cups.
- Chalkboard or newsprint with marker (Connect, Option 1).
- Pencils and index cards.
- Copy the handout (Connect, Option 2; Respond, Option 2).
- Bibles.
- If you are using actions with the Beatitudes, learn the actions for Matthew 5:6.
- If you are using Apply, Option 1, invite someone from your congregation who works for justice to talk about his or her work to your group.

EXPLORATION

FOCUS
(6-8 minutes)

Have you ever watched a food commercial on TV and developed such a craving for what was advertised that you immediately went to get the food and eat it? I remember watching cheese commercials that would not leave me alone until I had helped myself to a slice of cheese.

Bring one kind of snack food (cheese, chocolate, chips) and one kind of drink (with cups). Divide your class into two groups. Separate the groups so they cannot hear each other. Give the food item to one group and the drink to the other. Ask each group to create a commercial that will stimulate such a craving for their item that the group will not be content until every person has tasted the item.

After they present the commercials, ask the groups to share the food and drink with each other. While the food is being passed around, discuss: What was said or done that caused you to want the food or drink?

CONNECT
(4-8 minutes)

Option 1: a) Ask students to recall situations where they have been treated unfairly. Once they have situations in mind, ask: *What did it feel like to be treated unfairly? What did you do about it? Did anyone else do something about it?*

b) Ask students to recall situations where someone else was treated unfairly. Once they have situations in mind, ask: *Why did someone get treated unfairly? How did the person respond to the unfair treatment? Did anyone else do something about it?*

On the chalkboard or newsprint, make a list of pros and cons to getting involved when someone gets treated unfairly.

Option 2: Form groups of three or four and pass out the handout, "Confronting Injustice." Give students about five minutes to discuss with each other what they would likely do in these situations.

Transition comment: *Sometimes we are the victims of injustice while at other times we witness others being treated unfairly. We have two options when we witness oppression. We can remain silent and do nothing and become silent accomplices to the persecution. Or we can work against the injustice and risk our own safety. The way we respond may depend on how strongly we crave a better situation for others. We can increase our craving for justice when we desire God's righteousness for all people and when we learn from others who have passionately pursued justice on behalf of others.*

HEAR AND ENTER
(10-15 minutes)

Review the first three Beatitudes and learn Matthew 5:6, with or without the actions. Use whichever memorization method you prefer as described in Session 1 (Hear and Enter), with or without the actions shown at the back of this book.

Option 1: Rediscover the exciting story of Esther by dividing your teens into seven groups. Assign each group one chapter from the book of Esther beginning with chapter 2 and ending with chapter 8. Give the groups ten minutes to read their chapters and choose one person from the group to summarize the story for the rest of the class. Beginning with the chapter 2 group, have them briefly tell the story of Esther in sequence. (Note: If your group is too small for seven groups, you could divide them into three groups and assign chapters 2-3 to group A; chapters 4-6 to group B; and chapters 7-8 to group C.) The summary in Option 2 below can assist you as the groups tell the story of Queen Esther.

Option 2: Use the summary below in a TV reporter interview format by giving the questions to a member of the class and having them ask the questions in sequence as written. In order to be more dramatic, you could wear additional jewelry or find a robe to symbolize royalty.

Reporter: How did you become queen of Persia?

King Xerxes sent out commissioners throughout the land and told them to bring back the most beautiful women they could find. One of them would be chosen to be his wife. At the time, I was in the care of Mordecai, a cousin of my parents who had died. When I was asked to be part of this group, he told me not to reveal my family background and nationality. The king was attracted to me more than any of the other women, and after a year's time, I became his queen. Around the same time Mordecai uncovered a conspiracy to kill King Xerxes and I was able to prevent the assassination by informing the king of that plan (Esther 2).

Reporter: How did the plot to kill all the Jews come about?

Mordecai refused to kneel down and pay honor to Haman, an honored noble. When Haman found out Mordecai was a Jew, he devised a plan to kill not only Mordecai but all the Jews living in the land. He convinced King Xerxes to send out a decree to have all Jews killed on the thirteenth day of the twelfth month (Esther 3).

Reporter: How did you learn about this terrible plot?

One day I heard that Mordecai was sitting outside the King's Gate in sackcloth and ashes. When I sent a servant to find out the reason, I learned of Haman's plot. I wanted to beg for mercy on behalf of my people, but I knew that anyone who approached the king, including myself, without being summoned would be put to death. I decided that I had to do something, even at the risk of dying (Esther 4).

Reporter: Did you just go up to him and tell him about this plot?

No, I invited the king and Haman to a banquet. The king was eager to grant any request of mine, up to half the kingdom. In the meantime, Haman was so angered to see Mordecai that he made plans to have gallows built so he would be hung in the morning (Esther 5).

Reporter: So Esther's banquet was too late to save Mordecai's life?

Something else saved him. That night, King Xerxes could not sleep and had the record of his reign read to him. The reading reminded him that Mordecai had saved him from an assassination plot earlier in his reign. He honored him by giving him a royal robe and having Haman lead him on horseback through the city streets (Esther 6).

Reporter: What happened at the banquet?

I asked the king to grant me my life—and to spare my people. The king had no idea that I was a Jew and became angry with Haman. He ordered him to be hanged on the very gallows that Haman had prepared for Mordecai (Esther 7).

Reporter: Did it end there?

The king gave Haman's estate to me and placed Mordecai in charge of it. He then issued another decree that would allow Jews the right to assemble and protect themselves. This became a time of happiness and feasting for all the Jews (Esther 8).

Whether you use option 1 or 2, conclude this study by saying: *Queen Esther put herself at risk for her people. Since no one knew her background, she would have been spared in spite of the edict. However, her love for her people gave her a desire to do what she could to save them as well.*

APPLY
(10-15 minutes)

Option 1: Is there someone in your congregation who has a hunger for justice? a strong desire for righteousness? Is there someone who has worked hard to improve the rights of people who are disadvantaged? Invite this person to your class to talk about his or her activities and the reasons behind them. How have they experienced this craving for righteousness that Jesus talks about?

Option 2: Read the following story of a person who showed a deep concern for righteousness.

Martin Luther King, Jr., led the black American civil rights movement during the 1950s and 1960s. In some places during that time blacks could not attend the same schools as whites and were also required to sit at the back of a bus. Illegal acts such as lynchings of blacks were ignored and at times participated in by authorities.

King led the movement to end these injustices and others in a nonviolent way. He led boycotts against discriminatory institutions. He gave speeches and organized protests. A Baptist preacher by occupation, he led the March on Washington in 1963, one of the largest civil rights demonstrations ever. There he gave his most famous speech: "I Have a Dream." In that speech, he outlined his hope for a fair, equal, and just society. He wished that one day men and women of all races, religions, and cultures would join together and say, "Free at last! Free at last! Thank God Almighty, I'm free at last!" (Story by Jeremy)

Just as Martin Luther King, Jr., envisioned a more just world, and that vision guided and inspired his work, we too can envision a more just world.

Invite students to imagine a more just city or town than the one they live in. Ask them to close their eyes and picture possibilities as you direct the following questions to them: (Be sure to pause long enough after each question to allow students time to think and visualize.) *What kind of houses would people live in? What would they eat? How would they travel? How would people treat each other? What kind of laws would be enforced? What would happen when people broke the laws? How would people who are poor or disabled be treated? What kind of medical care would be available? How would children treat each other? What would school be like?*

After the imagination exercise has been completed, ask students to share their vision of a more just and righteous city or town.

Discuss:

Why is a vision of how things might be so important? (It gives us something concrete to strive for, a goal increases our desire to work towards achieving it.)

RESPOND
(5-10 minutes)

Option 1: Draw a box with the four areas on a chalkboard or newsprint.

Home	School
Church	"Out"

Ask: In which of these places do you find it hardest to "live right"—to treat others fairly and with respect?

Distribute index cards to each teen. Have them write the area that is most difficult to them on this card. Ask them to write one positive, specific thing they can do during the next week to make that place more just.

Option 2: Direct the students' attention to Part 2 of the handout, "Confronting Injustice." Go over the instructions. As a group, talk through how you would apply the three steps to Situation A. Then give the students a couple of minutes to write similar responses to Situations B and C. Ask for volunteers to share their answers.

Closing comment: *We hunger and thirst for something when we have developed a taste for it, when we have a sense that we are missing something. If we enjoy chips and cheese snacks and are used to eating them every weekend, what happens when the youth leader doesn't allow us to bring any to the weekend retreat? We develop such a* *craving that we will not be satisfied until we have eaten chips or cheese snacks after our arrival home. In the same way, God wants us to be so familiar with a society that is fair and just that whenever that picture is out of focus, we will not feel satisfied until it has been corrected.*

Closing prayer: Lead the group in praying the following serenity prayer by praying one phrase at a time and asking the class to repeat after you: *God, grant me the courage to change the things I can change, the serenity to accept those I cannot change, and the wisdom to know the difference. And, God, grant me the courage not to give up on what is right even though it may seem hopeless.*

REFLECT AND LOOK AHEAD

Did you communicate the importance of both doing what is right (treating others with dignity and respect) and standing up for others (when their needs are neglected or their rights abused)? To stand up for others takes courage. Fear of ridicule and rejection often immobilizes junior highs and keeps them from stepping forward. They may be willing to take such risks only if they are assured of the support of their close friends.

DIGGING DEEPER

Righteousness is a word that was full of meaning for the people of Jesus' time. The Old Testament prophets called people to righteous living. This did not mean that everyone was expected to be perfect. They were, however, to **strive** to be more loving, to **desire** to be more righteous. It meant not only treating others with respect and dignity, but also standing up for those who were being oppressed or treated unfairly by others.

HANDOUT

Confronting Injustice

Confronting *Injustice*

Part 1
In groups of three or four, discuss how you might respond to each of the situations described.

Situation A
You are in line at a fast-food restaurant when a person of color gets into the line next to you. Other people squeeze in near the front of the line. When the person of color ought to be served, the person behind the counter ignores this person and asks the next person, "How may I help you?" What would you do?

Situation B
Ken is being bullied by some bigger boys at school. Sometimes they just tease him. Other times they push him around. One day you see this going on. What would you do?

Situation C
You are part of a group hanging out in a hallway at school. Several kids start saying nasty and untrue things about Karen, who is not present. You know they are repeating false rumors. What would you do?

Part 2
Confronting others takes not only courage but skill as well. When someone does something that you feel is wrong, and it seems appropriate for you to be the one to confront him or her, here are some steps you can follow.

a) Look at the person.
b) Beginning your sentence with "I," describe what you are concerned about.
c) State the reason for your concern.

Using these three steps, write out an appropriate response to each of the three situations described above.

SESSION 5: HAVE MERCY

Preparation

Key verse: Blessed are the merciful, for they will receive mercy. (Matthew 5:7)

Faith focus: God calls us to be merciful—to feel with others and then respond to their needs with compassionate action. Those who show mercy to others will be shown God's mercy.

Session goal: Help your teens better understand how to feel with others, and encourage them to respond to the others with compassionate action.

Materials needed and advance preparation:
- Pencils.
- Chalkboard or newsprint and marker.
- Words written on small pieces of paper and placed in a container (Focus, Option 1).
- If you are using the actions for the Beatitudes, learn those for Matthew 5:7.
- Make copies of handouts. Prepare "Mime Match" strips as instructed in Focus, Option 1.

Exploration

FOCUS
(8-10 minutes)

Option 1: Make one copy of the "Mime Match" handout for each ten students in your group. (If you have twenty kids, make two copies.) Cut the strips apart, fold them with the words inside, and clip matching strips together. (Be careful not to confuse the "won" and "lost" football player strips.)

Once the group has gathered, count the group members. Then count out an equal number of strips and mix them in a hat or other container. (Take paper clips off.) Since this is a matching game, you need to have at least two of each strip used. If you have an odd number of teens that is fewer than ten, you can participate in the game to make an even number of players.

Have everyone stand. Tell them not to show anyone else their instructions. They are each to pantomime the character described on the slip of paper while looking around the room to find anyone else who is pantomiming the same thing. When they see someone else who they think is pantomiming the same thing, they are to go stand by the person, while continuing to play the character. When everyone is matched up, you will stop your miming and compare instructions to see if everyone made the right matches.

Option 2: Ask each person to find a partner whose feet are about the same size. Have them take off their own shoes and exchange them with the partner. Then ask them to walk in the other person's shoes for thirty seconds. Ask them to describe what it was like.

Then have partners tell each other where their own shoes have walked in the last twenty-four hours. After both partners have told their stories, ask if they would be willing to exchange places with each other for an entire day. Why or why not?

Return the shoes to the original owners and join together in one group.

CONNECT
(4-8 minutes)

It's interesting to try to "get inside the skin" (or shoes) of other people. We can never really know what it is like to be someone else, but it can be fun to imagine. Ask:

- *What makes it possible for us to see life from another person's point of view?*
- *What makes it hard to really get inside another person's skin?*
- *Can you think of anyone whose life you would like to live? Why?*
- *What is the value of trying to see life through another person's eyes?*

Transition comment: *Being able to feel another person's need or pain is the first step in becoming merciful people—and that's what today's Beatitude is about.*

HEAR AND ENTER
(10-15 minutes)

As a group, memorize Matthew 5:7, with or without the actions described in the back of the book. Review all five of the Beatitudes you have learned and repeat them until the entire class can recite them.

Divide your class into two groups. Ask each group to read through Matthew 18:23-34 (the parable of the unmerciful servant), then come up with a contemporary version of this parable they can act out for the group. After a few minutes have each group act out its parable for the class.

APPLY
(8-10 minutes)

If we want to become good at sensing what others feel and seeing through their eyes, we need to become skilled listeners. The two following options are designed to help teens improve their listening skills.

Option 1: Invite everyone to choose a partner. Have them decide who will be "A" and who will be "B." Then tell the B's that they will be the talkers and the A's will be the listeners. The B's are to tell the A's something important that has happened to them during the past week. The A's are to find ways to *not* listen. After a minute or so, ask the class to list the ways they became non-listeners. Write their answers on a chalkboard or newsprint. Possible answers:

- look around the room
- read
- talk to someone else
- walk away
- turn away
- interrupt

Next have the class identify and list good listening skills. Possible answers:

- look directly at the person who is talking
- sit or stand quietly while another is talking
- don't interrupt
- show you understand by nodding
- ask a question if you don't understood

Option 2: Pass out copies of the handout, "Listening So Others Feel Heard" to your class. Read the instructions at the top of that page and go over the first two examples with the class, then ask them to complete the final four on their own.

When the students are finished, review their

responses with them. There is no one right response to each statement. It's important that feelings be mentioned in the response. The following feelings and responses would be good listening responses:

3. Hassled. You feel hassled by Tim because he's always begging for money even though he has enough of his own.
4. Angry. You're angry with Janet for getting you in trouble during math class.
5. Annoyed. You're annoyed with your brother for not returning your music tapes.
6. Unfairly treated. It seems unfair to you that you have to do more than your share of the chores at home.

RESPOND
(3-6 minutes)

Option 1: Make sure group members all have pencil and paper, then lead them in a time of silent reflection.

Say: *Think about someone you know who is hurting. This person may be loud and obnoxious, strange or different, or quiet and shy. It may be a person who has problems at home or school, or who has recently suffered a loss.*

Make a list of six possible ways you might show mercy to this person—respond to his or her need with compassionate action. (Allow about ninety seconds for making lists.)

Which of the items on your list do you think would best show caring to this person? Do you need to talk to this person more, listen, get inside his or her skin, to be able to know what response would be most welcome? If so, how might you find or arrange an opportunity to spend some time talking and listening to him or her. Is this something you would like to do? If so, ask God to give you wisdom in knowing how best to approach this person, and sensitivity to the person's pain as you listen and choose how to respond with action. (Allow sixty seconds for silent prayer.)

Option 2: Say: It's easy to write people off—to stereotype them and ignore what they say, especially if they get on your nerves and make you angry. Think about such a person in your life. It may be a parent who is always lecturing you or a teacher who seems to be on your case constantly. Consider doing the following the next time you meet with this person:

- Look the person directly in the eyes and listen till they have finished.
- Listen to the words and think about what the person might be feeling.
- Summarize for the person what you heard and ask if you heard correctly.
- Ask the person to hear you out if you disagree or feel misunderstood.

Closing prayer: Say the following or a similar prayer. *Thank you for your mercy in our lives—for the many ways you reach out and care for us when we are weak or hurting. As a grateful response to your great mercy, empower us to be merciful to others. Help us to care enough to listen not only to people's words, but to the feelings behind them. Help us to translate our caring into compassionate action that reaches out and touches the hurt of others. Amen.*

REFLECT AND LOOK AHEAD

In today's study students have been challenged to enter more deeply into the lives of others. As they try to "walk in another's shoes" and understand each other better, they are taking steps toward becoming more merciful.

DIGGING DEEPER

Human mercy and divine mercy are closely related, according to this Beatitude. This theme is repeated many other places in the New Testament. In the Lord's Prayer, God's forgiveness depends on our forgiveness of others. The story of the unforgiving debtor shows that just as God forgives our great debts, we should forgive the smaller debts of others. Jesus appeals to us to be merciful to others as a response to the great mercy he has shown us.

What does it mean to be merciful? It is not just feeling sorry for someone. It means, first, to genuinely try to understand another from the other person's point of view. Seeing others through eyes of mercy isn't always easy. Being merciful may require us to give up prejudices or stereotypes, or get beyond our own anger or disappointment. But if we really want to see through another person's eyes, we can develop active listening skills that will take us a long way toward that goal.

But mercy, like understanding, doesn't stop. The Bible again and again speaks of showing mercy. Mercy is something we show, not just something we feel.

When, after coming to understand another's pain or need to some degree, we respond with compassionate action, we have become people who *show mercy.* Jesus promises that God will show mercy to those who show mercy.

HANDOUTS

Mime Match
Listening So Others Feel Heard

Mime Match

Photocopy this page and cut the strips apart. If your group is larger than ten, make enough copies for each group member to get a strip.

Using only actions, no sounds, pretend you are a four-year-old boy who fell down and skinned his knee.

Using only actions, no sounds, pretend you are a four-year-old boy who fell down and skinned his knee.

Using only actions, no sounds, pretend you are a ten-year-old girl whose kitten is sick.

Using only actions, no sounds, pretend you are a ten-year-old girl whose kitten is sick.

Using only actions, no sounds, pretend you are a football player whose team just won the Super Bowl.

Using only actions, no sounds, pretend you are a football player whose team just won the Super Bowl.

Using only actions, no sounds, pretend you are a football player whose team just lost the Super Bowl.

Using only actions, no sounds, pretend you are a football player whose team just lost the Super Bowl.

Using only actions, no sounds, pretend you are a teenager who woke up to find a big zit on your nose.

Using only actions, no sounds, pretend you are a teenager who woke up to find a big zit on your nose.

Listening So Others Feel Heard

For other people to feel heard, we must listen not only to their words, but also to the feelings behind their words.

Read the statement in the first column. In the second column identify a feeling the person making the statement might have had. In the third column, write a response you could make that would let the person know you heard both feelings and words. The first two have been completed for you as examples.

Person Says	Feeling	Listening Response
1. My parents have so many rules. All my friends can do whatever they want. I can't do anything. They treat me like a little kid.	frustration	You're frustrated with your parents because they have so many restricting rules.
2. Pamela is such a gossip. She's always telling lies about me. Lately she's been telling everyone that I copied her homework.	hurt	You feel hurt because of the rumors Pam is spreading about you.
3. Tim is always bugging me to give him money for bus fare. If he wouldn't spend his money in the cafeteria, he'd have enough to pay his own bus fare.		
4. I'm always getting into trouble because Janet talks to me during math class. I wish she would wait until after class to talk.		
5. I wish my brother would stop borrowing my music tapes. I can never find them when I want to listen to them.		
6. I always get stuck doing the chores around our house. My brother and sister seldom have to do anything.		

SESSION 6: HOW'S YOUR HEART CONDITION?

Preparation

Key verse: Blessed are the pure in heart, for they will see God. (Matthew 5:8)

Faith focus: To be pure in heart is to become singularly focused on God, not allow conflicting loyalties to blur our vision.

Session goal: Help teens become more aware of the motivations behind their actions, and encourage them to continually strive to be people whose actions are motivated by love for God and others.

Materials needed and advance preparation:
- If using Focus, Option 1, make and post motivation signs in your room beforehand.
- Blank paper (Focus, Option 2).
- Pencils.
- Bibles.
- Index cards.
- Learn the actions for Matthew 5:8 if you're using the actions.
- Make copies of handouts.

Exploration

FOCUS
(3-5 minutes)

Option 1: Play "Motivation Corner." Write each of the following four motivations on a separate sheet of paper with a felt marker:

My friends are doing it.
My parents told me to do it.
I think it's the best thing to do.
Because I want to.

Post the signs in the four corners of the room.

Read the actions listed below, one at a time. After reading each action, ask students to move to the corner that most closely describes their own motivation when they do the described action.

- You mow the lawn.
- You order a Coke at the pizza place.

- You phone your best friend.
- You complete a homework assignment.
- You practice your musical instrument.
- You go swimming.
- You go watch a movie.
- You clean your room.
- You read a book.
- You help at a school fund-raiser.
- You wear a red hat to school.
- You go to church.
- You change your socks.

Option 2: Form groups of three or four and give a blank piece of paper and a pencil to one person in each group. *Saturday Night Live* occasionally carries a speech with a subliminal message. These speeches often identify some of the hidden motives or secret thoughts behind actions and spoken words. Invite students to write a brief *Saturday-Night-Live*-style subliminal story [big joke]. Here's how such a story could be written:

It was the last day of camp [great week]. John had made many new friends [only guys]. All week he wanted to talk to Sally [scared stiff]. She seemed like such a friendly person [gorgeous] with a pleasant personality [very sexy]. If only he could get up enough courage to ask her to sit with him at the banquet tonight, his week would be perfect [cloud nine]. It would be an unforgettable evening sitting next to her, carrying on an interesting conversation [about sports and cars] with her. John waited for the time when she was alone [less embarrassing]. When he saw her sitting on a log near her cabin he felt the right moment [last chance] had arrived. Trying not to appear too eager [uncool], he casually [timidly] walked over to where she was sitting. Just as he approached her [point of no return], she looked up at him and smiled. There were a million things he wanted to say to her. He smiled back [tongue-tied]. "Hi!" he said and turned around [lost courage] and walked away.

It was the last day of camp [terrible week].

CONNECT
(4-8 minutes)

If you used Option 1: For some of the above actions (e.g., mow the lawn), the students may all have moved to the same corner (my parents told me to do it). For others (e.g., you go swimming), students may have had a variety of motives with some ending up in all four corners of the room. In still other situations, students may have had more than one motive. Perhaps they ordered a Coke because all of their friends were having Coke and because they really wanted to drink Coke.

For any action there are many other possible motives beyond the four listed above. Ask the class to think about other reasons for their actions. List their answers on a chalkboard or newsprint. Here are some possible answers:

- Because I'm getting paid.
- To gain a sense of accomplishment.
- To complete something I started.
- Because I care about my friend.
- To receive affirmation.
- To make this world a better place.
- To please God.
- Because I don't want to pay a fine.
- Because I have no other options.

To evaluate motives, we must ask whether our motives lead to loving actions. Do they help us to do what is right? Go back to the motives you listed on the chalkboard and see if you can tell whether they lead us to do what God wants us to do. (You will find that many of the motives are neutral in and of themselves. In other words, they are closely tied to the action and therefore must be evaluated together with the action.)

If you used Option 2: Have the teens read their stories to each other. Talk about the gap between what we often say and what we are thinking.

•**Discuss as a class:** *Why is it important to be aware of the gap between our thoughts and our actions?* (To serve God, it is important that our desires not conflict with obeying God.)

Transition comment: *We have many reasons for our actions. We may be aware of some reasons and unaware of others. In today's Beatitude, we will learn that God cares about our reasons for our actions and looks for a heart motivated by love.*

HEAR AND ENTER
(8-12 minutes)

Teach the class Matthew 5:8 using any of the memorization methods. Review the other Beatitudes you have learned until the entire class can recite them. If you wish, use the accompanying actions shown at the back of the book.

Pass out Bibles, pencils, and the handout, "What

the Bible Says About Being Pure." Working individually, in pairs or small groups, have students look up these passages and complete the two blank columns. Then discuss their findings. Below are some possible answers.

a) Job 4:17 (to be pure is to be righteous)
b) Psalm 24:4 (to be pure is to not serve an idol)
c) Psalm 119:9 (to stay pure, live according to God's Word)
d) Habakkuk 1:13 (pure eyes do not look upon evil or tolerate wrong)
e) Philippians 1:10 (to be pure is to discern what is best)
f) Philippians 4:8 (pure is equated with that which is true, noble, right, lovely, admirable, excellent and praiseworthy)
g) 1 Timothy 5:22 (keep yourself pure by not sharing in the sins of others)
h) 2 Timothy 2:22 (a pure heart pursues righteousness, faith, love, and peace)

APPLY
(8-10 minutes)

Option 1: Pass out index cards and ask each person to write down something he or she has recently done or committed to do. Fill out a card yourself. Then write on the chalkboard or newsprint:

Motive Checklist
- Why am I doing this?
- Does it show love to others? If so, how?
- Will it please God? How do I know?

Tell what you wrote on your card, then answer the three questions about your activity. Then call on another person in the class, explaining that he or she can answer the same three questions about what is on his or her card, or may pass. Either way, the person then calls on someone else in the class to answer the same three questions. Everyone has the option to pass, but the person who passes still chooses the next one to answer. Continue until everyone has had a chance to share or until you run short on time.

Ask: *Were any of you surprised by your own answers to your questions? Did you have motives for doing your activi-*

ty that you hadn't been aware of before? What would you do if you concluded that your motive was not pleasing to God?

Option 2: Share the following story of a child's pure motivation that saved a family's life.

In 1917 a reign of terror began in Russia. Bandits went around the country robbing and killing people wherever they went.

In the Russian Mennonite homes, there was a tradition around Christmas that children would learn a Bible verse and recite it to their family. If this was done well, they would receive a little bit of money for it. This was called their Christmas money.

It was late one night around Christmas when the dog at the Klassen house started barking. They knew the bandits were coming. In a few minutes the bandits were in the house demanding money. When Father Klassen told them they had no money, the bandits coldly replied, "Then we will have to shoot you."

Then a little girl about nine or ten said, "I will get you my Christmas money." She left the room and when she came back, there in her hands were a few small coins.

There was complete silence in the room. One of the bandits bent over and kissed the girl on her forehead. One by one they left silently and nothing more was taken that night.

By offering what she had, the little Klassen girl saved her family. She didn't do it for brownie points. She gave it sincerely from her heart. (Story by Rachel, based on a story in *Peace Be With You* by Cornelia Lehn, copyright 1980 by Faith & Life Press.)

Ask, *Who do you know who is "pure in heart?" What have you observed that makes you believe this person is "pure in heart"?*

RESPOND
(8-10 minutes)

Pass out the handout, "Top Ten Motives to Avoid When Doing a Good Deed." Have students work in groups of two or three to complete their lists. The whole group can work on one list, or they can help each other fill out individual lists. Have group members read their lists to the class.

Closing prayer: On the back of a handout (or a blank sheet of paper), invite students to write a short prayer about being pure in heart. Collect the prayers and end the class by reading the prayers anonymously.

REFLECT AND LOOK AHEAD

Are the teens in your group more aware of their motives? Do they see value in being in touch with the reasons for their actions? Will this awareness lead them to loving actions that are pleasing to God?

DIGGING DEEPER

According to Hebrew teaching, there is a close connection between one's motives and actions. Actions grow out of motives. The constant challenge for the Christian is to be singularly focused on God so that conflicting loyalties do not prevent loving actions.

Sometimes "pure in heart" is translated to mean we ought to have "clean thoughts." That may be good advice for the Christian, but this Beatitude expects more than developing a clean mind.

Those with pure hearts are those who want what is right. They want what God wants and will evaluate their motives on the basis of whether it is pleasing to God and loving towards others. Since motives are closely related to actions, we do well to monitor them and evaluate them on basis of the actions that result from them.

It only follows that persons who are singularly focused on God will see God. We see what we are trained to see. Someone who does not understand music may see a page of notes. Someone trained to read music will see a song. As we keep our eyes focused on God, we will see God more clearly, and follow God more nearly.

HANDOUTS

What the Bible Says About Being Pure
Top Ten Motives to Avoid When Doing a Good Deed

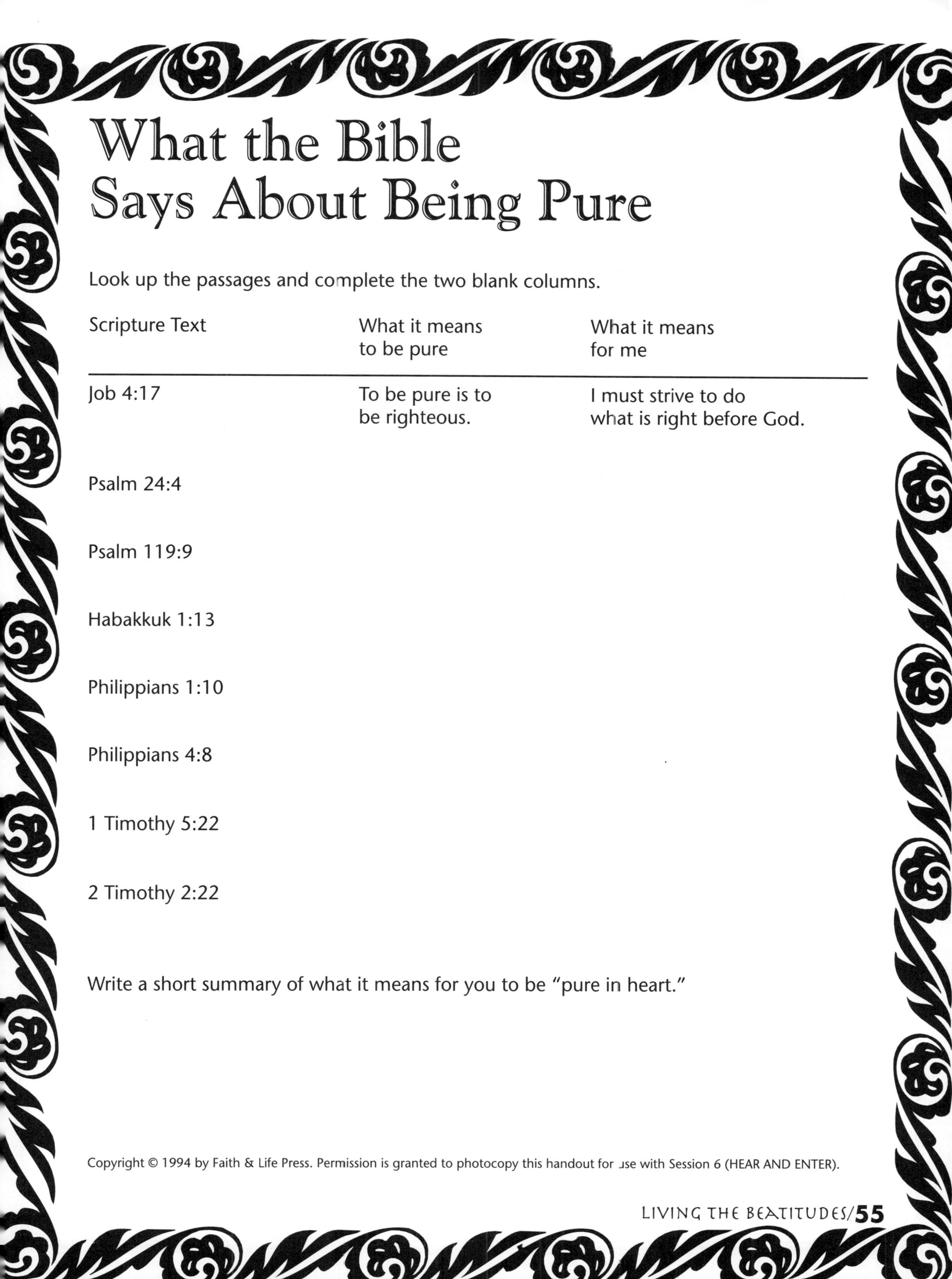

What the Bible Says About Being Pure

Look up the passages and complete the two blank columns.

Scripture Text	What it means to be pure	What it means for me
Job 4:17	To be pure is to be righteous.	I must strive to do what is right before God.
Psalm 24:4		
Psalm 119:9		
Habakkuk 1:13		
Philippians 1:10		
Philippians 4:8		
1 Timothy 5:22		
2 Timothy 2:22		

Write a short summary of what it means for you to be "pure in heart."

TOP TEN

Motives to Avoid When Doing a Good Deed

10. ______________________________

9. ______________________________

8. ______________________________

7. ______________________________

6. ______________________________

5. ______________________________

4. ______________________________

3. ______________________________

2. I may get nominated for the Nobel Peace Prize.

1. My parents might reward me by buying me a TV and VCR for my room.

SESSION 7: ME, A PEACEMAKER?

PREPARATION

Key verse: Blessed are the peacemakers, for they will be called children of God. (Matthew 5:9)

Faith focus: Christians are called to strive for peace in all aspects of life—in personal relationships, between nations, and throughout the entire creation.

Session goal: Help students understand that they are each called to be peacemakers and realize they can help to bring peace to their world.

Materials needed and advance preparation:

- Bibles.
- Pencils.
- Video camera, VCR, monitor (Hear and Enter, Option 2, optional).
- Index cards (Respond, Option 3).
- Make copies of handouts.
- Learn the movement for this Beatitude if you are using actions.

EXPLORATION

FOCUS
(5-8 minutes)

From the following list of statements, choose about ten that seem most suited to your class. Read them one-by-one as students express their agreement or disagreement as follows:

Agree—raise hand
Strongly agree—wave hand
Disagree—thumb down
Strongly disagree—shake thumb
No opinion—fold arms across chest

How many of you:
•Believe God wants people to live at peace?

- Think world peace could become a reality in the future?
- Feel it's a Christian's duty to bring about peace in our world?
- Think it is more difficult to live at peace with your family than with your friends?
- Think that war is always wrong?
- Believe that Christians should work at peace mainly in their personal relationships?
- Think pacifism works in the real world?
- Believe that youth can help to bring about peace in the world?
- Feel that the best way to secure peace is to have everyone mind their own business?
- Believe that God wants Christians to be active peacemakers?
- Feel that Christians and non-Christians can work together effectively in peace efforts?
- Believe Christians should make their beliefs about peace known to governments?
- Feel peace is emphasized too much in your church?
- Feel that there can be no real peace until injustices have been made right?
- Believe that when the Bible talks about peace, it is referring only to inner peace?

After you have gone through the list of ten statements, go back to two or three statements where you noticed diversity of opinion and invite students to explain their opinions.

CONNECT
(3-5 minutes)

Ask: *Have you ever been treated with violence? What happened? Have you ever witnessed violence in person? Can you describe it? Why do you think there is more violence in our society than there used to be?*

Transition comment: *Christians have different opinions about the importance of peace. Some feel that an inner peace with God is what's most important. Others feel that peace within relationships is where the emphasis ought to be. Still others would like to see all Christians working more actively against war and violence. What does the Bible teach about this issue?*

As a group, memorize this Beatitude. Review the other six Beatitudes and repeat them until the entire class can recite verse 3 through 8 in order, with or without the accompanying actions.

HEAR AND ENTER
(5-10 minutes)

Option 1: Many stories in the Bible illustrate peacemaking. Three stories in Genesis each illustrate an important peacemaking principle. Choose one of the stories, or have your class divide into three groups and assign one story to each group. Ask them to read the story(ies) and summarize in one or two sentences what this story teaches about making peace.

a) Abraham and Lot (Genesis 13—Abraham makes peace by giving up his right to have the best land.)
b) Jacob and Esau (Genesis 32:1-21—Jacob restores his relationship with Esau by acknowledging how he wronged him in the past and trying to compensate him for that.)
c) Joseph and his brothers (Genesis 45:1-8—Joseph forgives his brothers when he realizes they have changed their ways and now want to protect each other.)

Option 2: One of Jesus' most difficult teachings is found in Luke 6:27-36 where he tells his followers to "love your enemies." Our natural inclination is to hate our enemies. Jesus, however, shows another way—he challenges us to turn our enemies into neighbors. That's what happened in the story of the good Samaritan. Jews and Samaritans hated each other. But that all changed when a Samaritan helped an "enemy" in need. Since this is likely a familiar story, divide your class into two groups and ask them each to come up with a modern version of the story.

To add interest, you may want to borrow a video camera from a church member and then videotape the two dramas so you can watch them later.

APPLY
(8-12 minutes)

Option 1: Read the following story to your group. Ask them as a group to come up with an ending that shows peacemaking in action.

Janet began eighth grade at the top of her class. Soon she found herself in competition with a popular classmate. Susan also did very well in class, but could not quite achieve the same marks as Janet. She was jealous and so did her best to exclude Janet from all social groups at school. Because Susan talked negatively about her, others began to treat Janet badly. Janet responded to the rejection by eating until she was quite a bit overweight. This only made things worse for her as she not only felt lonely and isolated, but her self-image fell even further.

One day . . . (complete the story).

Option 2: Ask students if they can think of any situations they have encountered in the past month that lacked peace. Brainstorm ideas for bringing peace to these situations.

Option 3: Invite a peace activist to your class to talk about his or her involvements and to suggest ways for your group to become involved in peacemaking.

Optional: After completing one of the above options, you may want to share the following story:

Ever since the time of Abraham, the Arabs and the Jews have been considered "blood brothers." Elias Chacour was seven years old when his "blood brothers" came to his town of Biram. His father told him that the soldiers would be carrying guns, but not to be afraid because "they are our brothers." When the soldiers arrived, a feast of lamb was prepared for them.

Several days later the leader of the soldiers told Elias' father that the town of Biram was in danger so they should evacuate it for a few days. Within the same day the people of Biram packed their things and were on their way out of the town.

Months went by and there was still no sign of the soldiers telling them they could return. After more months of waiting, the people decided to go back home. When they got to Biram, they found the first house with the door smashed in and everything inside was stolen. The same had happened to all the other houses.

When the leader of the soldiers saw that the people had returned, he leveled his gun at them and turned off the safety switch. "Get out!" he yelled, "this is our town now."

How can I ever feel peace with my neighbors again? Elias thought when he heard this. Elias' father saw the anger in his son's eyes and said to him, "They are our brothers. We must forgive them." (Story by Rachel)

RESPOND
(5-10 minutes)

Option 1: Pass out pencils and the "Peace Machine" handout. Give the group members about five minutes to make their drawings, then ask them to show and explain them.

Option 2: Play a version of *Pictionary* using the words below. You could divide the group into two teams and organize a friendly competition between the teams. Or you could set a time limit of thirty seconds per person.

Instructions: Invite one person from each team and show them one word only. Their task is to go back to their team and draw the word for the team. The first team to guess the right word wins a point. If you use the time limit option, the team wins a point if they guess the word within the allotted time.

Words to use: *army, dove, gun, television, pray, world, enemy, love, peace.*

After each word discuss how it relates to peace.

Option 3: Distribute an index card to each person. Ask each one to write down one thing he or she can do to make the world a more peaceful place.

Closing prayer: Pass out the "Prayer of St. Francis" handout. Close the session by reading the prayer together. You may want to ask all to memorize the prayer.

REFLECT AND LOOK AHEAD

Do your teens understand that God expects us to become peacemakers in every area of our lives? Do they have a sense that there are things they can do to help bring about peace?

DIGGING DEEPER

The Hebrew word for peace is shalom. It means more than the absence of war. It is used to describe physical well-being. Jacob asks Joseph to check on the shalom of his brothers (Genesis 37:14). Frequently it refers to good relationships between people, groups, and nations.

Even if there is no open conflict, there is no shalom when injustices are present. If parents favor one child over the other, there will be no harmony in the home. When people are treated unfairly, they may resort to violence to try to remedy the situation. All relationships ought to be life-giving, healthy, and fair.

God wants peace for the entire world. God hopes that everyone in the world will be at peace with God, with each other, and even with creation.

God not only wants peace for our world, but is working to bring it about. Many of God's peacemaking efforts are carried on through the people who have chosen to serve God. In this Beatitude, those who help to bring about peace are called "children of God."

Sometimes we use the phrase, *like father, like son,* or

like mother, like daughter. Children take on the qualities and characteristics of their parents. They may walk like them or have similar interests or values. Peacemakers are called children of God because they have taken on the concerns and qualities of God.

HANDOUTS

Peace Machine
Prayer of St. Francis

Peace MACHINE

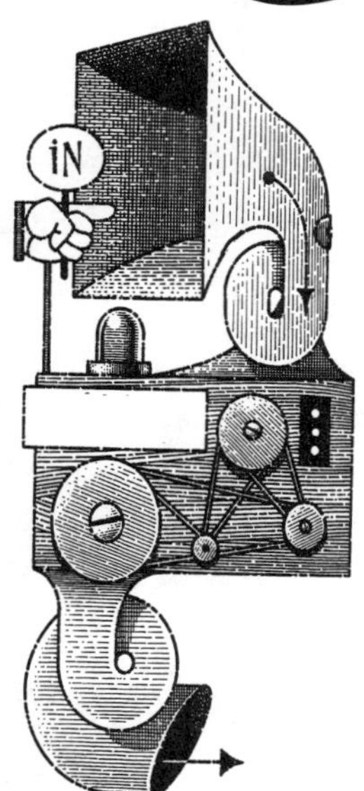

You have just invented a machine that will bring peace to people and nations. Complete the drawing of the machine on this page and then explain to your group how it works.

Prayer of St. Francis

Lord, make me an instrument of your peace.
Where there is hatred, let me sow love.
Where there is injury, pardon.
Where there is doubt, faith.
Where there is despair, hope.
Where there is darkness, light.
Where there is sadness, joy.

O Divine Master, grant that I may not so much seek
to be consoled as to console;
to be understood, as to understand;
to be loved, as to love.
For it is in giving that we receive.
It is in pardoning that we are pardoned.
And it is in dying that we are born to eternal life.

Amen.

—St. Francis of Assisi

SESSION 8:

PREPARATION

Key verse: Blessed are those who are persecuted for righteousness' sake, for theirs is the kingdom of heaven. (Matthew 5:10)

Faith focus: God calls Christians to stand up for what is right even when there is a price to pay.

Session goal: Identify pressures that make it tempting to compromise convictions and encourage students to stand up for what's right regardless of the price they have to pay.

Materials needed and advance preparation:

- Matches, and one candle for every ten students (Focus, Option 2).
- Legal size (11 x 14" or 27.5 x 35 cm.) sheets of paper and colored markers (Respond, Option 1).
- Lined paper/pen (Respond, Option 2).
- Chalkboard or newsprint and marker.
- Copy and cut apart handout (Focus, Option 1).
- Learn actions for Matthew 5:10, if you're using the actions.
- Write out sentence prayers to be used during closing prayer time if you think they will be needed (Respond).

EXPLORATION

FOCUS
(4-8 minutes)

Option 1: Form groups of three to five. Give each group a situation from the "Choices Under Pressure" handout. Give them three minutes to decide what they would do. After the time is up, ask someone from each group to read their particular situation and tell what they decided to do.

Option 2: For this activity you will need about nine or ten participants. If your group is larger than that, divide them into groups of that size. Each group should form a gauntlet—half of the participants on one side and the other half on the other side, facing each other about seven feet apart. Each person holding a lit candle must try to make it through the gauntlet without that light being extinguished. As soon as the person with the candle starts moving, those in the two lines can try to blow out the candle without moving their feet, though they are allowed to bend over to try to blow out the candle. Give everyone a chance to make it through with a lit candle. After each person's attempt, he or she will exchange places with someone in one of the two lines.

CONNECT
(4-8 minutes)

If you chose Option 1 above, discuss:

In which of the four situations would it be the most difficult to do the right thing? Why?

Can you describe a similar situation you have been in where it was tough to do the right thing?

What helped you (would help you) to do what is right when the pressure to go along with the crowd is great?

If you chose Option 2 above, discuss:

What was it like trying to make it through this hostile territory without getting your candle blown out? (It was impossible, didn't have a chance, wasn't fair.)

What was it like being in one of the two lines? (It was fun, easy, no challenge.)

How was this activity like real life? (At times it's hard letting your light shine; trying to be a witness can be a lonely experience; it's easy to go along with the crowd.)

What can we learn from this activity? (As Christians we need to support each other; it's important to develop some strategies that allow our lights to shine.)

Transition comment: *There are times when everyone finds it difficult to stand up for what is right. Pressures or ridicule can make us afraid to do what we know is right. Many Bible characters faced opposition from others around them. How did they handle these situations?*

HEAR AND ENTER
(10-15 minutes)

Lead the group in memorizing Matthew 5:10. Review the other seven Beatitudes and as a group recite them all in order, using the actions if you wish. You might also call out specific verse references (for example, "5:5") and have students quote the verse as quickly as they can.

Option 1: As a class, recount the story of Joseph (Genesis chapters 37, 38-45) from memory. Be sure the following stories are not forgotten: his brother's throwing him in a pit and selling him into slavery, the attempted seduction and accusations by Potiphar's wife, imprisonment, forgotten in prison. Though Joseph tried to do what was right, he seemed to continually get into trouble. When you have finished telling the story, discuss:

What helped Joseph to pull through tough times? (He sensed that God was with him, knew he was doing right, never lost hope that things would get better.)

List some of the blessings Joseph experienced as a result of his commitment to do what was right. (People recognized his integrity and gave him responsibilities; his relationship to God was deepened; God used him to save his family and others.)

Option 2: Read the story of Daniel's three friends—Shadrach, Meshach, and Abednego (Daniel 3). Ask students to mime the story as you read it. After you have completed the chapter, discuss:

What gave them the courage to stand firm for their beliefs? (Their trust in God, support of each other, knowing they were doing right.)

APPLY
(5-8 minutes)

Option 1: To stand firm during times of pressure and persecution, a helpful skill is to learn to say no assertively. Write the following four steps on chalkboard or newsprint.

Saying No Assertively

- Look at the person.
- In a clear, firm voice, say: "No, I don't want to...."
- If the person persists, ask him or her to leave you alone.
- Remain calm but serious.

Invite several students to practice this skill by taking part in a role-play with you. Tell them you will pressure them to do something. They should respond firmly and assertively as suggested on the chalkboard.

a) Let's go have a smoke. (pause) Don't be a sissy; it's not going to kill you.
b) I think we should rent this X-rated movie. (pause) There's nothing in here we haven't seen before.

c) I know a place where it's easy to steal a few chocolate bars. (pause) It's a big store; they'll never miss a few bars.

d) Let's find out what's on the test. I know where the teacher keeps the exams. (pause) It's no big deal, we probably know most of the stuff anyway.

Option 2: Read or ask a student to read the following story to your group.

El Salvador is a Central American country ruled by military dictatorship. Opposing the government often results in murder.

El Salvador is mostly Roman Catholic, but it has a deep division within. On one side is the hierarchy (priests, bishops and archbishops) and on the other side is the Popular People's Church. The hierarchy is supported by the military and is very conservative. The Popular People's Church is run mostly by priests and nuns. They have the people's support and are opposed to the military government. Such views are dangerous to communicate.

Oscar Romero was appointed archbishop because of his conservative views. However, when he saw how the government treated the poor and violated human rights, he spoke out against the government. Thus he became more of a spokesman for the Popular Church. His sermons attacked the government and were broadcast on radio. Archbishop Romero was martyred by an assassin's bullet in March of 1980 while saying mass. (Story by Jeremy)

After the story is read, ask the students if they know of any people who have been persecuted for their faith. Invite them to share these stories.

RESPOND
(10-15 minutes)

Option 1: When we reflect on the lives of Joseph or Daniel's friends, we notice that they had some things in common when facing difficult times. Working in groups of two or three, have the students create posters with the following six words that summarize three keys that helped these men prevail under pressure:

Know Right
Stand Firm
Keep Hope

Pass out legal size paper and colored markers for this activity.

Option 2: In many countries people are unjustly held as prisoners because they have been working to achieve greater freedom and human rights in their country. As a class, write a letter to: Amnesty International, Canadian Section, 214 Montreal Rd, Suite 401, Vanier, ON K1P 9Z9 (Attention: Youth Campus Network) or Amnesty International, US Section, 322 Eighth Avenue, New York NY 10001 (Attention: Youth Campus Network) to learn about some of these persons who are unjustly imprisoned. Find out ways you can support them.

Closing prayer: Have the group stand and form a circle. Explain that as a group, you will say each of the Beatitudes in turn, pausing after each one for a prayer response. If you have learned the motions to the Beatitudes, use them as you say the Beatitudes together. If you are not using the motions, hold hands for the prayer.

For the prayer responses to each Beatitude, you may ask students to volunteer with an appropriate one-sentence prayer after each Beatitude. For example, in response to "Blessed are the poor in spirit, for theirs is the kingdom of heaven," someone might say, "God, help us to realize more and more how much we need you."

If you don't think this would work with your group, you could pray a sentence prayer in response to each Beatitude, or you could write out sentence prayers before class and pass them out to students to be read after the related Beatitude.

After reciting all eight Beatitudes and responding with sentence prayers to each, conclude by reciting together a prayer you all know, such as the Lord's Prayer, the Prayer of St. Francis, or a prayer song that is meaningful to your group.

REFLECT

We have completed our study of the Beatitudes. Do your students have a better idea of what it means to enter the kingdom of God? Have you seen evidence that some have taken steps along the spiritual stairway? The Beatitudes call us to self-examination and to action. In the process we are born anew as children of God.

DIGGING DEEPER

One possible outcome of living faithfully as a child of God is persecution. People will oppose the way of righteousness in three ways: ridicule, persecution, and slander. This opposition keeps us dependent on God (poor in spirit) as we realize that we cannot do it alone. We need God's constant presence and other believers' support and encouragement when the going gets tough.

HANDOUT

Choices Under Pressure

Choices Under PRESSURE

Photocopy the situation descriptions below and cut them apart for use in Focus, Option 1. Give each group a copy of one of the situations below. What would they do if they faced this difficult choice?

Your parents went out of town leaving you and your older sister (age 17) home alone. They clearly said, "no parties" while they were gone. A few of your friends would like to get together at your place. That wouldn't be a party, would it? You are worried that things will get out of hand and that others who were not invited will drop by. If you don't let them come, everyone will be mad at you. What would you do?

You agreed to go to a movie with some friends. When you get to the theater, you find that the movie you wanted to see is sold out. Your friends want to go to the X-rated one playing nearby. They tell you it will be no problem getting in, even though you are under age. What do you do?

Lately your girlfriend has been wearing some very revealing outfits. You are uncomfortable with that and feel that if you don't talk about it soon, you may not be getting together very much in the future. What would you do?

A few of your friends are at another friend's house. While checking the cupboard for some snacks, they notice several bottles of liquor in the same cupboard. Some of the bottles are open and someone suggests that everyone try some. What would you do?

APPENDIX

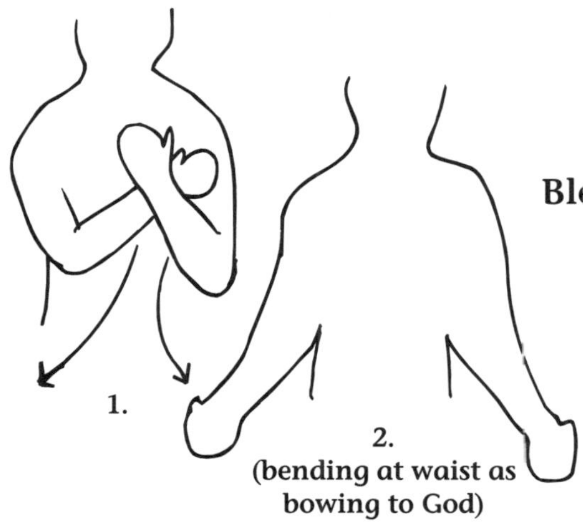

Blessed are the poor in spirit,

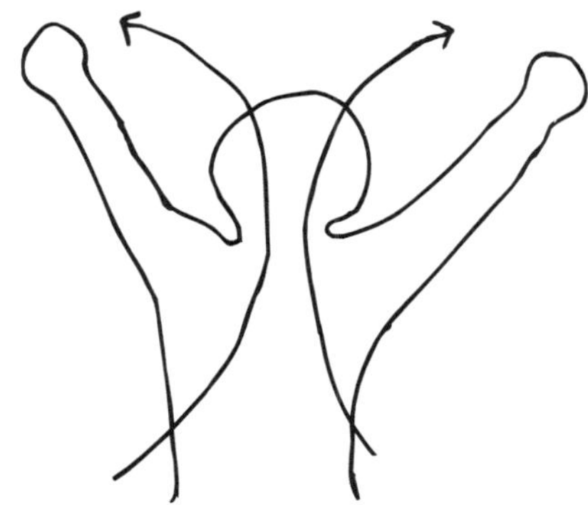

for theirs is the kingdom of heaven.

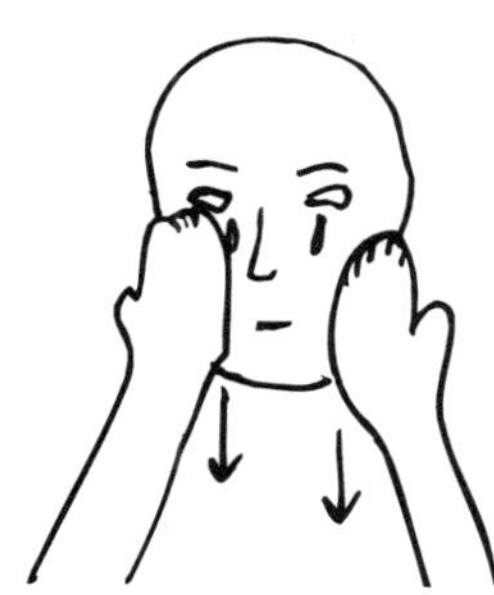

Blessed are those who mourn,

for they will be comforted

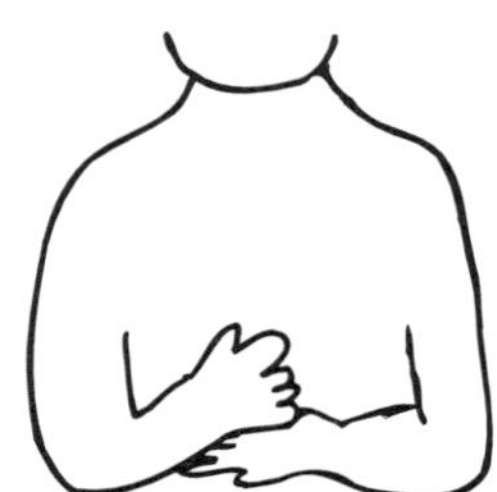

Blessed are the meek,

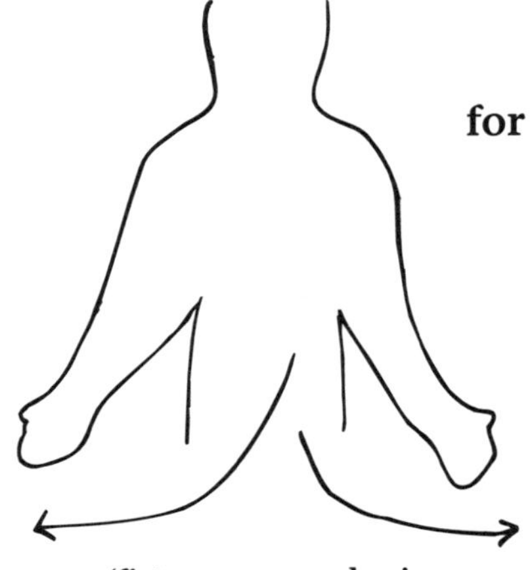

for they will inherit the earth.

(fist on open palm in middle of stomach)

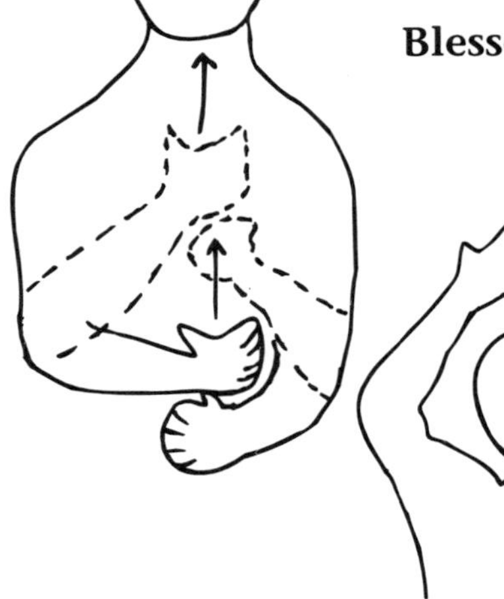

Blessed are those who hunger and thirst

for righteousness,

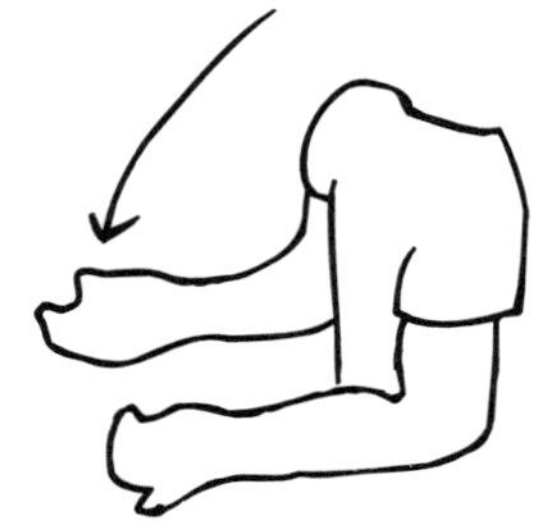

for they will be filled.

Blessed are the merciful,

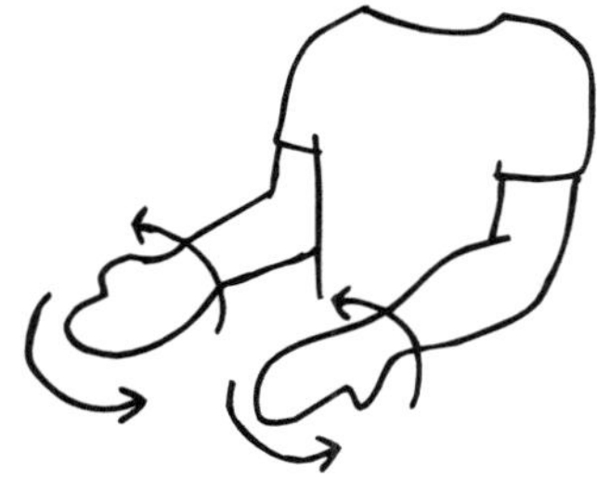

for they will receive mercy.

Blessed are the pure in heart,

for they will see God.

Blessed are the peacemakers,

for they will be called the children of God.

Blessed are those who are persecuted for righteousness' sake,

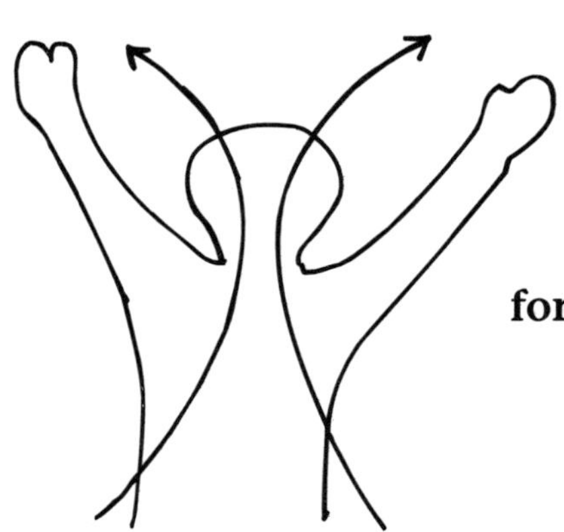

for theirs is the kingdom of heaven.

(stand)